Bankruptcy
BASICS

Leonidas Ralph Mecham, Director

Administrative Office
of the United States Courts

Bankruptcy
BASICS

Public Information Series

Bankruptcy Judges Division

Administrative Office
of the United States Courts

APRIL 2004
Revised Second Edition

Table of CONTENTS

Bankruptcy BASICS

A Public Information Series of the Bankruptcy Judges Division

THE PAMPHLET

The Bankruptcy Judges Division's Public Information Series pamphlet provides basic information to debtors, creditors, court personnel, the media, and the general public on different aspects of the federal bankruptcy laws. The series is also designed to provide individuals who may be considering bankruptcy with a basic explanation of the different chapters under which a bankruptcy case may be filed and to answer some of the most commonly asked questions about the bankruptcy process.

This pamphlet provides general information only. While every effort has been made to ensure that the information contained in it is accurate as of the date of publication, it is not a full and authoritative statement of the law on any particular topic. The information presented in the pamphlet should not be cited or relied upon as legal authority and should not be used as a substitute for reference to the United States Bankruptcy Code (title 11, United States Code) and the Federal Rules of Bankruptcy Procedure.

Most importantly, the pamphlet should not substitute for the advice of competent legal counsel or a financial expert. Neither the Bankruptcy Judges Division nor the Administrative Office of the United States Courts can provide legal or financial advice. Such advice may be obtained from a competent attorney, accountant, or financial adviser.

THE PROCESS

Article I, Section 8, of the United States Constitution authorizes Congress to enact "uniform Laws on the subject of Bankruptcies." Under this grant of authority, Congress enacted the "Bankruptcy Code" in 1978. The Code, which is codified as title 11 of the United States Code, has been amended several times since its enactment. It is the uniform federal law that governs all bankruptcy cases.

The procedural aspects of the bankruptcy process are governed by the Federal Rules of Bankruptcy Procedure (often called the "Bankruptcy Rules") and local rules of bankruptcy. The Bankruptcy Rules contain a set of official forms for use in bankruptcy cases. The Bankruptcy Code and Bankruptcy Rules (and local rules) set forth the formal legal procedures for dealing with the debt problems of individuals and businesses.

There is a bankruptcy court for each judicial district in the country. Each state has one or more districts. There are 90 bankruptcy districts across the country. The bankruptcy courts generally have their own clerk's offices.

> The court official with decision-making power over federal bankruptcy cases is the United States bankruptcy judge, a judicial officer of the United States district court.

The court official with decision-making power over federal bankruptcy cases is the United States bankruptcy judge, a judicial officer of the United States district court. The bankruptcy judge may decide any matter connected with a bankruptcy case, such as eligibility to file or whether a debtor should receive a discharge of debts. Much of the bankruptcy process is administrative, however, and is conducted away from the courthouse. In cases under chapter 7, 12, or 13, and sometimes in chapter 11 cases, this administrative process is carried out by a trustee who is appointed to oversee the case.

A debtor's involvement with the bankruptcy judge is usually very limited. A typical chapter 7 debtor will not appear in court and will not see the bankruptcy judge unless an objection is raised in the case. A chapter 13 debtor may only have to appear before the bankruptcy judge at a plan confirmation hearing. Usually, the only formal proceeding at which a debtor must appear is the meeting of creditors, which is usually held at the offices of the United States trustee. This meeting is informally called a "341 meeting" because section 341 of the Bankruptcy Code requires that the debtor attend this meeting so that creditors can question the debtor about debts and property.

A fundamental goal of the federal bankruptcy laws enacted by Congress is to give debtors a financial "fresh start" from burdensome debts. The Supreme Court made this point about the purpose of the bankruptcy law in a 1934 decision:

> [I]t gives to the honest but unfortunate debtor...a new opportunity in life and a clear field for future effort, unhampered by the pressure and discouragement of preexisting debt.

Local Loan v. Hunt, 292 U.S. 234, 244 (1934). This goal is accomplished through the bankruptcy discharge, which releases debtors from personal liability from specific debts and prohibits creditors from ever taking any action against the debtor to collect those debts. This pamphlet describes the **Discharge in Bankruptcy** in a question and answer format, discussing the timing of the discharge, the scope of the discharge (what debts are discharged and what debts are not discharged), objections to discharge, and revocation of the discharge. It also describes what a debtor can do if a creditor attempts to collect a discharged debt after the bankruptcy case is concluded.

There are five basic types of bankruptcy cases provided for under the Bankruptcy Code, each of which is discussed in this pamphlet. The cases are traditionally given the names of the chapters that describe them.

Chapter 7, entitled Liquidation, contemplates an orderly, court-supervised procedure by which a trustee collects the assets of the debtor's estate, reduces them to cash, and makes distributions to creditors, subject to the debtor's right to retain certain exempt property and the rights of secured creditors. Because there is usually little or no nonexempt property in most chapter 7 cases, there may not be an actual liquidation of the debtor's assets. These cases are called "no-asset cases." A creditor holding an unsecured claim will get a distribution from the bankruptcy estate only if the case is an asset case and the creditor files a proof of claim with the bankruptcy court. In most chapter 7 cases, the debtor receives a discharge that releases the debtor from personal liability for certain dischargeable debts. The debtor normally receives a discharge just a few months after the petition is filed.

Chapter 13, entitled Adjustment of Debts of an Individual With Regular Income, is designed for an individual debtor who has a regular source of income. Chapter 13 is often preferable to chapter 7 because it enables the debtor to keep a valuable asset, such as a house. It is also favored because it allows the debtor to propose a "plan" to repay creditors over time—usually three to five years. At a confirmation hearing, the court either approves or disapproves the plan, depending on whether the plan meets the Bankruptcy Code's requirements for confirmation. Chapter 13 is very different from chapter 7, since the chapter 13 debtor usually remains in possession of the property of the estate and makes payments to creditors, through the trustee, based on the debtor's anticipated income over the life of the plan. Unlike chapter 7, the debtor does not receive an immediate discharge of debts. The debtor must complete the payments required under the plan before the discharge is received. The debtor is protected from lawsuits, garnishments, and other creditor action while the plan is in effect. The discharge is also considerably broader (i.e., more debts are eliminated) under chapter 13 than the discharge under chapter 7.

Chapter 11, entitled Reorganization, ordinarily is used by commercial enterprises that desire to continue operating a business and repay creditors concurrently through a court-approved plan of reorganization. The chapter 11 debtor has the exclusive right to file a plan of reorganization for the first 120 days after the order for relief and must provide creditors with a disclosure statement containing information adequate to enable creditors to evaluate the plan. The court ultimately approves (confirms) or disapproves the plan of reorganization. Under the confirmed plan, the debtor can reduce its debts by repaying a portion of its obligations and discharging others. The debtor can also terminate burdensome contracts and leases, recover assets, and rescale its operations in order to return to profitability. Under chapter 11, the debtor normally goes through a period of consolidation and emerges with a reduced debt load and a reorganized business.

Chapter 12, entitled Adjustment of Debts of a Family Farmer with Regular Annual Income, provides debt relief to family farmers with regular annual income. The process under chapter 12 is very similar to that of chapter 13 under which the debtor proposes a plan to repay debts over a period of time— no more than three years unless the court approves a longer period, not exceeding five years. There is also a trustee in every chapter 12 case whose duties are very similar to those of a chapter 13 trustee. The chapter 12 trustee's disbursement of payments to creditors under a confirmed plan parallels the procedure under chapter 13. Chapter 12 allows a family farmer to continue to operate the farm while the plan is being carried out.

Chapter 9, entitled Adjustment of Debts of a Municipality, provides essentially for reorganization, much like a reorganization under chapter 11. Only a "municipality" may file under chapter 9, which includes cities and towns, as well as villages, counties, taxing districts, municipal utilities, and school districts.

This pamphlet also contains a description of liquidation proceedings under the Securities Investor Protection Act. Although the Bankruptcy Code provides for a stockbroker liquidation proceeding, it is far more likely that a failing brokerage firm will find itself involved in a SIPA proceeding. The purpose of SIPA is to return to investors securities and cash left with failed brokerages.

Since being established by Congress in 1970, the Securities Investor Protection Corporation has protected investors who deposit stocks and bonds with brokerage firms by ensuring that every customer's property is protected, up to $500,000 per customer.

The bankruptcy process is complex and relies on legal concepts like the "automatic stay," "discharge," "exemptions," and "substantial abuse." Therefore, the final chapter of this booklet is a glossary of Bankruptcy Terminology which explains, in layman's terms, most of the legal concepts that apply in cases filed under the Bankruptcy Code.

The Discharge in Bankruptcy

DISCHARGE

The bankruptcy discharge varies depending on the type of case a debtor files: chapter 7, 11, 12, or 13. This Public Information Series pamphlet attempts to answer some basic questions about the discharge available to individual debtors under all four chapters including:

1. What is a discharge in bankruptcy?

2. When does the discharge occur?

3. How does the debtor get a discharge?

4. Are all the debtor's debts discharged or only some?

5. Does the debtor have a right to a discharge or can creditors object to the discharge?

6. Can the debtor receive a second discharge in a later chapter 7 case?

7. Can the discharge be revoked?

8. May the debtor pay a discharged debt after the bankruptcy case has been concluded?

9. What can the debtor do if a creditor attempts to collect a discharged debt after the case is concluded?

10. May an employer terminate a debtor's employment solely because the person was a debtor or failed to repay a discharged debt?

From an individual debtor's standpoint, one of the primary goals of filing a bankruptcy case is to obtain relief from burdensome debt. Relief is attained through the bankruptcy discharge, the purpose of which is to provide a "fresh start" to the honest debtor.

WHAT IS A DISCHARGE IN BANKRUPTCY?

Under the federal bankruptcy statute, a discharge is a release of the debtor from personal liability for certain specified types of debts. In other words, the debtor is no longer required by law to pay any debts that are discharged. The discharge operates as a permanent order directed to the creditors of the debtor that they refrain from taking any form of collection action on discharged debts, including legal action and communications with the debtor, such as telephone calls, letters, and personal contacts.

Although a debtor is relieved of personal liability for all debts that are discharged, a valid lien (i.e., a charge upon specific property to secure payment of a debt) that has not been avoided (i.e., made unenforceable) in the bankruptcy case will remain after the bankruptcy case. Therefore, a secured creditor may enforce the lien to recover the property secured by the lien.

WHEN DOES THE DISCHARGE OCCUR?

The timing of the discharge varies, depending on the chapter under which the case is filed. In a chapter 7 (liquidation) case, for example, the court usually grants the discharge promptly on expiration of the time fixed for filing a complaint objecting to discharge and the time fixed for filing a motion to dismiss the case for substantial abuse (60 days following the first date set for the 341 meeting). Typically, this occurs about four months after the date the debtor files the petition with the clerk of the bankruptcy court. In chapter 11 (reorganization) cases, the discharge occurs upon confirmation of a chapter 11 plan. In cases under chapter 12 (adjustment of debts of a family farmer) and 13 (adjustment of debts of an individual with regular income), the court grants the discharge as soon as practicable after the debtor completes all payments under the plan. Since a chapter 12 or chapter 13 plan may provide for payments to be made over three to five years, the discharge typically occurs about four years after the date of filing.

HOW DOES THE DEBTOR GET A DISCHARGE?

Unless there is litigation involving objections to the discharge, the debtor will automatically receive a discharge. The Federal Rules of Bankruptcy Procedure provide for the clerk of the bankruptcy court to mail a copy of the order of discharge to all creditors, the United States trustee, the trustee in the case, and the trustee's attorney, if any. The debtor and the debtor's attorney also receive copies of the discharge order. The notice, which is simply a copy of the final order of discharge, is not specific as to those debts determined by the court to be non-dischargeable, i.e., not covered by the discharge. The notice informs creditors generally that the debts owed to them have been discharged and that they should not attempt any further collection. They are cautioned in the notice that continuing collection efforts could subject them to punishment for contempt. Any inadvertent failure on the part of the clerk to send the debtor or any creditor a copy of the discharge order promptly within the time required by the rules does not affect the validity of the order granting the discharge.

ARE ALL OF THE DEBTOR'S DEBTS DISCHARGED OR ONLY SOME?

Not all debts are discharged. The debts discharged vary under each chapter of the Bankruptcy Code. Section 523(a) of the Code specifically excepts various categories of debts from the discharge granted to individual debtors. Therefore, the debtor must still repay those debts after bankruptcy. Congress has determined that these types of debts are not dischargeable for public policy reasons (based either on the nature of the debt or the fact that the debts were incurred due to improper behavior of the debtor, such as the debtor's drunken driving).

There are 18 categories of debt excepted from discharge under chapters 7, 11, and 12. A more limited list of exceptions applies to cases under chapter 13.

Generally speaking, the exceptions to discharge apply automatically if the language prescribed by section 523(a) applies. The most common types of non-dischargeable debts are certain types of tax claims, debts not set forth by the debtor on the lists and schedules the debtor must file with the court, debts for spousal or child support or alimony, debts for willful and malicious injuries to person or property, debts to governmental units for fines and penalties, debts for most government funded or guaranteed educational loans or benefit overpayments, debts for personal injury caused by the debtor's operation of a motor vehicle while intoxicated, and debts for certain condominium or cooperative housing fees.

The types of debts described in sections 523(a)(2), (4), (6), and (15) (obligations affected by fraud or maliciousness or certain debts incurred in connection with property settlements arising out of

> Under the federal bankruptcy statute, a discharge is a release of the debtor from personal liability for certain specified types of debts. In other words, the debtor is no longer required by law to pay any debts that are discharged.

a separation agreement or divorce decree) are not automatically excepted from discharge. Creditors must ask the court to determine that these debts are excepted from discharge. In the absence of an affirmative request by the creditor and subsequent granting of the request by the court, the types of debts set out in sections 523(a)(2), (4), (6), and (15) will be discharged.

A broader discharge of debts is available to a debtor in a chapter 13 case than in a chapter 7 case. As a general rule, the chapter 13 debtor is discharged from all debts provided for by the plan except certain long-term obligations (such as a home mortgage), debts for alimony or child support, debts for most government funded or guaranteed educational loans or benefit overpayments, debts arising from death or personal injury caused by driving while intoxicated or under the influence of drugs, and debts for restitution or a criminal fine included in a sentence on the debtor's conviction of a crime. Although a chapter 13 debtor

> A governmental unit or private employer may not discriminate against a person solely because the person was a debtor, was insolvent before or during the case, or has not paid a debt that was discharged in the case.

generally receives a discharge only after completing all payments required by the court-approved (i.e., "confirmed") repayment plan, there are some limited circumstances under which the debtor may request the court to grant a "hardship discharge" even though the debtor has failed to complete plan payments. Such a discharge is available only to a debtor whose failure to complete plan payments is due to circumstances beyond the debtor's control.

The scope of a chapter 13 "hardship discharge" is similar to that in a chapter 7 case with regard to the types of debts that are excepted from the discharge. A hardship discharge also is available in chapter 12 if the failure to complete plan payments is due to "circumstances for which the debtor should not justly be held accountable."

DOES THE DEBTOR HAVE THE RIGHT TO A DISCHARGE OR CAN CREDITORS OBJECT TO THE DISCHARGE?

In chapter 7 cases, the debtor does not have an absolute right to a discharge. An objection to the debtor's discharge may be filed by a creditor, by the trustee in the case, or by the United States trustee. Creditors receive a notice shortly after the case is filed that sets forth much important information, including the deadline for objecting to the discharge. A creditor who desires to object to the debtor's discharge must do so by filing a complaint in the bankruptcy court before the deadline set out in the notice. Filing of a complaint starts a lawsuit referred to in bankruptcy as an "adversary proceeding." A chapter 7 discharge may be denied for any of the reasons described in section 727(a) of the Bankruptcy Code, including the transfer or concealment of property with intent to hinder, delay, or defraud creditors; destruction or concealment of books or records; perjury and other fraudulent acts; failure to account for the loss of assets; violation of a court order; or an earlier discharge in a chapter 7 or 11 case commenced within six years before the date the petition was filed. If the issue of the debtor's right to a discharge goes to trial, the objecting party has the burden of proving all the facts essential to the objection.

In chapter 12 and chapter 13 cases, the debtor is entitled to a discharge upon completion of all payments under the plan. The Bankruptcy Code does not provide grounds for objecting to the discharge of a chapter 12 or chapter 13 debtor. Creditors can object to confirmation of the repayment plan, but cannot object to the discharge if the debtor has completed making plan payments.

CAN A DEBTOR RECEIVE A SECOND DISCHARGE IN A LATER CHAPTER 7 CASE?

A discharge will be denied in a later chapter 7 case if the debtor has been granted a discharge under chapter 7 or chapter 11 in a case filed within six years before the second petition is filed. The debtor will also be denied a chapter 7 discharge if he or she previously was granted a discharge in a chapter 12 or chapter 13 case filed within six years before the date of the filing of the second case unless (1) all the "allowed unsecured" claims in the earlier case were paid in full, or (2) payments under the plan in the earlier case totaled at least 70 percent of the allowed unsecured claims and the debtor's plan was proposed in good faith and the payments represented the debtor's best effort.

CAN THE DISCHARGE BE REVOKED?

A discharge can be revoked under certain circumstances. For instance, a trustee, creditor, or the United States trustee may request that the court revoke the debtor's discharge in a chapter 7 case based on allegations that the debtor obtained the discharge fraudulently; the debtor failed to disclose the fact that he or she acquired or became entitled to acquire property that would constitute property of the bankruptcy estate; or the debtor committed one of several acts of impropriety described in section 727(a)(6) of the Bankruptcy Code. Typically, a request to revoke the debtor's discharge must be filed within one year after the granting of the discharge or, in some cases, before the date that the case is closed. It is up to the court to determine whether such allegations are true and, if so, to revoke the discharge.

In a chapter 13 case, if confirmation of a plan or the discharge is obtained through fraud, the court can revoke the order of confirmation or discharge.

MAY THE DEBTOR PAY A DISCHARGED DEBT AFTER THE BANKRUPTCY CASE HAS BEEN CONCLUDED?

A debtor who has received a discharge may voluntarily repay any discharged debt. A debtor may repay a discharged debt even though it can no longer be legally enforced. Sometimes a debtor agrees to repay a debt because it is owed to a family member or because it represents an obligation to an individual for whom the debtor's reputation is important, such as a family doctor.

WHAT CAN THE DEBTOR DO IF A CREDITOR ATTEMPTS TO COLLECT A DISCHARGED DEBT AFTER THE CASE IS CONCLUDED?

If a creditor attempts collection efforts on a discharged debt, the debtor can file a motion with the court, reporting the action and asking that the case be reopened to address the matter. The bankruptcy court will often do so to ensure that the discharge is not violated. The discharge constitutes a permanent statutory injunction prohibiting creditors from taking any action, including the filing of a lawsuit, designed to collect a discharged debt. A creditor can be sanctioned by the court for violating the discharge injunction. The normal sanction for violating the discharge injunction is civil contempt, which is often punishable by a fine.

CAN AN EMPLOYER TERMINATE A DEBTOR'S EMPLOYMENT SOLELY BECAUSE THE PERSON WAS A DEBTOR OR FAILED TO REPAY A DISCHARGED DEBT?

The law provides express prohibitions against discriminatory treatment of debtors by both governmental units and private employers. A governmental unit or private employer may not discriminate against a person solely because the person was a debtor, was insolvent before or during the case, or has not paid a debt that was discharged in the case. The law prohibits the following forms of governmental discrimination: terminating an employee; discriminating with respect to hiring; or denying, revoking, suspending, or declining to renew a license, franchise, or similar privilege. A private employer may not discriminate with respect to employment if the discrimination is based solely upon the bankruptcy filing.

Liquidation Under the Bankruptcy Code

Chapter 7 of the United States Bankruptcy Code is the Bankruptcy Code's "liquidation" chapter. Lawyers sometimes refer to it as a "straight bankruptcy." It is used primarily by individuals who wish to free themselves of debt simply and inexpensively, but may also be used by businesses that wish to liquidate and terminate their business.

ALTERNATIVES TO CHAPTER 7

Debtors should be aware that there are several alternatives to chapter 7 relief. For example, debtors who are engaged in business, including corporations, partnerships, and sole proprietorships, may prefer to remain in business and avoid liquidation. Such debtors should consider filing a petition under chapter 11 of the Bankruptcy Code. Under chapter 11, the debtor may seek an adjustment of debts, either by reducing the debt or by extending the time for repayment, or may seek a more comprehensive reorganization. Sole proprietorships may also be eligible for relief under chapter 13 of the Bankruptcy Code.

In addition, individual debtors who have regular income may seek an adjustment of debts under chapter 13 of the Bankruptcy Code. Indeed, the court may dismiss a chapter 7 case filed by an individual whose debts are primarily consumer rather than business debts if the court finds that the granting of relief would be a substantial abuse of the provisions of chapter 7. 11 U.S.C. § 707(b). A number of courts have concluded that a chapter 7 case may be dismissed for substantial abuse when the debtor has the ability to propose and carry out a workable and meaningful chapter 13 plan.

Debtors should also be aware that out-of-court agreements with creditors or debt counseling services may provide an alternative to a bankruptcy filing.

BACKGROUND

The potential chapter 7 debtor should understand that a straight bankruptcy case does not involve the filing of a plan of repayment as in chapter 13, but rather envisions the bankruptcy trustee's gathering and sale of the debtor's nonexempt assets, from which holders of claims (creditors) will receive distributions in accordance with the provisions of the Bankruptcy Code. Part of the debtor's property may be subject to liens and mortgages that pledge the property to other creditors. In addition, under chapter 7, the individual debtor is permitted to retain certain "exempt" property. The debtor's remaining assets are liquidated by a trustee. Accordingly, potential debtors should realize that the filing of a petition under chapter 7 may result in the loss of property.

In order to qualify for relief under chapter 7 of the Bankruptcy Code, the debtor must be an individual, a partnership, or a corporation. 11 U.S.C. §§ 109(b); 101(41). Relief is available under chapter 7 irrespective of the amount of the debtor's debts or whether the debtor is solvent or insolvent. An individual cannot file under chapter 7 or any other chapter, however, if during the preceding 180 days a prior bankruptcy petition was dismissed due to the debtor's willful failure to appear before the court or comply with orders of the court or the debtor voluntarily dismissed the previous case after creditors sought relief from the bankruptcy court to recover property upon which they hold liens. 11 U.S.C. §§ 109(g), 362(d) and (e).

One of the primary purposes of bankruptcy is to discharge certain debts to give an honest individual debtor a "fresh start." The discharge has the effect of extinguishing the debtor's personal liability on dischargeable debts. In a chapter 7 case, however, a discharge is available to individual debtors only, not to partnerships or corporations. 11 U.S.C. § 727(a)(1). Although the filing of an individual chapter 7 petition usually results in a discharge of debts, an individual's right to a discharge is not absolute, and some types of debts are not discharged. Moreover, a bankruptcy discharge does not extinguish a lien on property.

HOW CHAPTER 7 WORKS

A chapter 7 case begins with the debtor's filing a petition with the bankruptcy court.[1] The petition should be filed with the bankruptcy court serving the area where the individual lives or where the business debtor has its principal place of business or principal assets. 28 U.S.C. § 1408. In addition to the petition, the debtor is also required to file with the court several schedules of assets and liabilities, a schedule of current income and expenditures, a statement of financial affairs, and a schedule of executory contracts and unexpired leases. Bankruptcy Rule 1007(b). A husband and wife may file a joint petition or individual petitions. 11 U.S.C. § 302(a). (Official Bankruptcy Forms can be purchased at a legal stationery store. They are not available from the court.)

In order to complete the Official Bankruptcy Forms which make up the petition and schedules, the debtor(s) will need to compile the following information:

1. A list of all creditors and the amount and nature of their claims;

2. The source, amount, and frequency of the debtor's income;

3. A list of all of the debtor's property; and

4. A detailed list of the debtor's monthly living expenses, i.e., food, clothing, shelter, utilities, taxes, transportation, medicine, etc.

Currently, the courts are required to charge a $155 case filing fee, a $39 miscellaneous administrative fee, and a $15 trustee surcharge (a total of $209). The fees should be paid to the clerk of the court upon filing or may, with the court's permission, be paid by individual debtors in installments. 28 U.S.C. § 1930(a); Bankruptcy Rule 1006(b); Bankruptcy Court Miscellaneous Fee Schedule, Item 8. Rule 1006(b) limits to four the number of installments for the filing fee. The final installment shall be payable not later than 120 days after filing the petition. For cause shown, the court may extend the time of any installment, provided that the last installment is paid not later than 180 days after the filing of the petition. Bankruptcy Rule 1006(b). The $39 administrative fee and the $15 trustee surcharge may be paid in installments in the same manner as the filing fee. If a joint petition is filed, only one filing fee, one administrative fee, and one trustee surcharge are charged. Debtors should be aware that failure to pay these fees may result in dismissal of the case. 11 U.S.C. § 707(a).

The filing of a petition under chapter 7 "automatically stays" most actions against the debtor or the debtor's property. 11 U.S.C. § 362. This stay arises by operation of law and requires no judicial action. As long as the stay is in effect, creditors generally cannot initiate or continue any lawsuits, wage garnishments, or even telephone calls demanding payments. Creditors normally receive notice of the filing of the petition from the clerk.

One of the schedules that will be filed by the individual debtor is a schedule of "exempt" property. Federal bankruptcy law provides that an individual debtor[2] can protect some property from the claims of creditors either because it is exempt under federal bankruptcy law or because it is exempt under the laws of the debtor's home state. 11 U.S.C. § 522(b). Many states have taken advantage of a provision in the bankruptcy law that permits each state to adopt its own exemption law in place of the federal exemptions. In other jurisdictions, the individual debtor has the option of choosing between a federal package of exemptions or exemptions available under state law. Thus, whether certain property is exempt and may be kept by the debtor is often a question of state law. Legal counsel should be consulted to determine the law of the state in which the debtor lives.

A "meeting of creditors" is usually held 20 to 40 days after the petition is filed. If the United States trustee or bankruptcy administrator[3] designates a place for the meeting that is not regularly staffed by the United States trustee or bankruptcy administrator, the meeting may be held no more than 60 days after the order for relief. Bankruptcy Rule 2003(a). The debtor must attend this meeting, at which creditors may appear and ask questions regarding the debtor's financial affairs and property. 11 U.S.C. § 343. If a husband and wife have filed a joint petition, they both must attend the creditors' meeting. The trustee also will attend this meeting. It is important for the debtor to cooperate with the trustee and to provide any financial records or documents that the trustee requests. The trustee is required to examine the debtor orally at the meeting of creditors to ensure that the debtor is aware of the potential consequences of seeking a discharge in bankruptcy, including the effect on credit history, the ability to file a petition under a different chapter, the effect of receiving a discharge, and the effect of reaffirming a debt. In some courts, trustees may provide written information on these topics at or in advance of the meeting, to ensure that the debtor is aware of this information. In order to preserve their independent judgment, bankruptcy judges are prohibited from attending the meeting of creditors. 11 U.S.C. § 341(c).

In order to accord the debtor complete relief, the Bankruptcy Code allows the debtor to convert a chapter 7 case to either a chapter 11 reorganization case or a case under chapter 13,[4] as long as the debtor meets the eligibility standards under the chapter to which the debtor seeks to convert, and the case has not previously been converted to chapter 7 from either chapter 11 or chapter 13. Thus, the debtor will not be permitted to convert the case repeatedly from one chapter to another. 11 U.S.C. § 706(a).

ROLE OF THE CASE TRUSTEE

Upon the filing of the chapter 7 petition, an impartial case trustee is appointed by the United States trustee (or by the court in Alabama and North Carolina) to administer the case and liquidate the debtor's nonexempt assets. 11 U.S.C. §§ 701, 704. If, as is often the case, all of the debtor's assets are exempt or subject to valid liens, there will be no distribution to unsecured creditors. Typically, most chapter 7 cases involving individual debtors are "no asset" cases. If the case appears to be an "asset" case at the outset, however, unsecured creditors[5] who have claims against the debtor must file their claims with the clerk of court within 90 days after the first date set for the meeting of creditors. Bankruptcy Rule 3002(c). In the typical no asset chapter 7 case, there is no need for creditors to file proofs of claim. If the trustee later recovers assets for distribution to unsecured creditors, creditors will be given notice of that fact and additional time to file proofs of claim. Although secured creditors are not required to file proofs of claim in chapter 7 cases in order to preserve their security interests or liens, there may be circumstances when it is desirable to do so. A creditor in a chapter 7 case who has a lien on the debtor's property should consult an attorney for advice.

The commencement of a bankruptcy case creates an "estate." The estate technically becomes the temporary legal owner of all of the debtor's property. The estate consists of all legal or equitable interests of the debtor in property as of the commencement of the case, including property owned or held by another person if the debtor has an interest in the property. Generally speaking, the debtor's creditors are paid from nonexempt property of the estate.

The primary role of a chapter 7 trustee in an "asset" case is to liquidate the debtor's nonexempt assets in a manner that maximizes the return to the debtor's unsecured creditors. To accomplish this, the trustee attempts to liquidate the debtor's nonexempt property, i.e., property that the debtor owns free and clear of liens and the debtor's property which has market value above the amount of any security interest or lien and any exemption that the debtor holds in the property. The trustee also pursues causes of action (lawsuits) belonging to the debtor and pursues the trustee's own causes of action to recover money or property under the trustee's "avoiding powers." The trustee's avoiding powers include the power to set aside preferential transfers made to creditors within 90 days before the petition, the power to undo security interests and other prepetition transfers of property that were not properly perfected under nonbankruptcy law at the time of the petition, and the power to pursue nonbankruptcy claims such as fraudulent conveyance and bulk transfer remedies available under state law. In addition, if the debtor is a business, the bankruptcy court may authorize the trustee to operate the debtor's business for a limited period of time, if such operation will benefit the creditors of the estate and enhance the liquidation of the estate. 11 U.S.C. § 721.

The distribution of the property of the estate is governed by section 726 of the Bankruptcy Code, which sets forth the order of payment of all claims. Under section 726, there are six classes of claims, and each class must be paid in full before the next lower class is paid anything. The debtor is not particularly interested in the trustee's disposition of the estate assets, except with respect to the payment of those debts

> Upon the filing of the chapter 7 petition, an impartial case trustee is appointed by the United States trustee (or by the court in Alabama and North Carolina) to administer the case and liquidate the debtor's nonexempt assets.

which for some reason are not dischargeable in the bankruptcy case. The debtor's major interests in a chapter 7 case are in retaining exempt property and in getting a discharge that covers as many debts as possible.

DISCHARGE

A discharge releases the debtor from personal liability for discharged debts and prevents the creditors owed those debts from taking any action against the debtor or his property to collect the debts. The bankruptcy law regarding the scope of a chapter 7 discharge is complex, and debtors should consult competent legal counsel in this regard prior to filing. As a general rule, however, excluding cases which are dismissed or converted, individual debtors receive a discharge in more than 99 percent of chapter 7 cases. In most cases, unless a complaint has been filed objecting to the discharge or the debtor has filed a written waiver, the discharge will be granted to a chapter 7 debtor relatively early in the case, that is, 60 to 90 days after the date first set for the meeting of creditors. Bankruptcy Rule 4004(c).

The grounds for denying an individual debtor a discharge in a chapter 7 case are very narrow and are construed against a creditor or trustee seeking to deny the debtor a chapter 7 discharge. Among the grounds for denying a discharge to a chapter 7 debtor are that the debtor failed to keep or produce adequate books or financial records; the debtor failed to explain satisfactorily any loss of assets; the debtor committed a bankruptcy crime such as perjury; the debtor failed to obey a lawful order of the bankruptcy court; or the debtor fraudulently transferred, concealed, or destroyed property that would have become property of the estate. 11 U.S.C. § 727; Bankruptcy Rule 4005.

In certain jurisdictions, secured creditors may retain some rights to seize pledged property, even after a discharge is granted. Depending on individual circumstances, a debtor wishing to keep possession of the pledged property, such as an automobile, may find it advantageous to "reaffirm" the debt. A reaffirmation is an agreement between the debtor and the creditor that the debtor will pay all or a portion of the money owed, even though the debtor has filed bankruptcy. In return, the creditor promises that, as long as payments are made, the creditor will not repossess or take back the automobile or other property. Because there is a disagreement among the courts concerning whether a debtor whose debt is not in default may retain the property and pay under the original contract terms without reaffirming the debt, legal counsel should be consulted to ensure that the debtor's rights are protected and that any reaffirmation is in the debtor's best interest.

If the debtor elects to reaffirm the debt, the reaffirmation should be accomplished prior to the granting of a discharge. A written agreement to reaffirm a debt must be filed with the court and, if the debtor is not represented by an attorney, must be approved by the judge. 11 U.S.C. § 524(c). The Bankruptcy Code requires that reaffirmation agreements contain an explicit statement advising the debtor that the agreement is not required by bankruptcy or nonbankruptcy law. In addition, the debtor's attorney is required to advise the debtor of the legal effect and consequences of such an agreement, including a default under such an agreement. The Code requires a reaffirmation hearing only if the debtor has not been represented by an attorney during the negotiating of the agreement. 11 U.S.C. § 524(d). The debtor may repay any debt voluntarily, however, whether or not a reaffirmation agreement exists. 11 U.S.C. § 524(f).

Most claims against an individual chapter 7 debtor are discharged. A creditor whose unsecured claim is discharged may no longer initiate or continue any legal or other action against the debtor to collect the obligation. A discharge under chapter 7, however, does not discharge an individual debtor from certain specific types of debts listed in section 523 of the Bankruptcy Code. Among the types of debts which are not discharged in a chapter 7 case are alimony and child maintenance and support obligations, certain taxes, debts for certain educational benefit overpayments or loans made or guaranteed by a governmental unit, debts for willful and malicious injury by the debtor to another entity or to the property of another entity, debts for death or personal injury caused by the debtor's operation of a motor vehicle while the debtor was intoxicated from alcohol or other substances, and debts for criminal restitution orders under title 18, United States Code. 11 U.S.C. § 523(a). To the extent that these types of debts are not fully paid in the chapter 7 case, the debtor is still responsible for them after the bankruptcy case has concluded. Debts for money or property obtained by false pretenses, debts for fraud or defalcation while acting in a fiduciary capacity, debts for willful and malicious injury by the debtor to another entity or to the property of another entity, and debts arising from a property settlement agreement incurred during or in connection with a divorce or separation are discharged unless a creditor timely files and prevails in an action to have such debts declared excepted from the discharge. 11 U.S.C. § 523(c); Bankruptcy Rule 4007(c).

The court may revoke a chapter 7 discharge on the request of the trustee, a creditor, or the United States trustee if the discharge was obtained through fraud by the debtor or if the debtor acquired property that is property of the estate and knowingly and fraudulently failed to report the acquisition of such property or to surrender the property to the trustee. 11 U.S.C. § 727(d).

NOTES

1. An involuntary chapter 7 case may be commenced under certain circumstances by the filing of a petition by creditors holding claims against the debtor. 11 U.S.C. § 303.

2. Each debtor in a joint case (both husband and wife) can claim exemptions under the federal bankruptcy laws. 11 U.S.C. § 522(m).

3. United States trustees and bankruptcy administrators are responsible for establishing a panel of private trustees to serve as trustees in chapter 7 cases and for supervising the administration of cases and trustees in cases under chapters 7, 11, 12, and 13 of the Bankruptcy Code. Bankruptcy administrators serve in the judicial districts in the states of Alabama and North Carolina.

4. A fee of $645 is charged for converting, on request of the debtor, a case under chapter 7 to a case under chapter 11. There is no fee for converting from chapter 7 to chapter 13.

5. Unsecured debts generally may be defined as those for which the extension of credit was based purely upon an evaluation by the creditor of the debtor's ability to pay, as opposed to secured debts, for which the extension of credit was based upon the creditor's right to seize pledged property on default, in addition to the debtor's ability to pay.

CHAPTER 13

Individual Debt Adjustment

Chapter 13 of the
United States Bankruptcy
Code is frequently referred
to as a "wage earner"
chapter, although it is
available to individuals
with regular income
from any source, not
just wages.

BACKGROUND

Chapter 13 is designed for individuals with regular income who desire to pay their debts but are currently unable to do so. The purpose of chapter 13 is to enable financially distressed individual debtors, under court supervision and protection, to propose and carry out a repayment plan under which creditors are paid over an extended period of time. Under this chapter, debtors are permitted to repay creditors, in full or in part, in installments over a three-year period, during which time creditors are prohibited from starting or continuing collection efforts. A plan providing for payments over more than three years must be "for cause" and be approved by the court. In no case may a plan provide for payments over a period longer than five years. 11 U.S.C. § 1322(d).

Any individual, even if self-employed or operating an unincorporated business, is eligible for chapter 13 relief as long as the individual's unsecured debts are less than $307,675 and secured debts are less than $922,975. 11 U.S.C. § 109(e). A corporation or partnership may not be a chapter 13 debtor. Id.

An individual cannot file under chapter 13 or any other chapter if, during the preceding 180 days, a prior bankruptcy petition was dismissed due to the debtor's willful failure to appear before the court or comply with orders of the court or was voluntarily dismissed after creditors sought relief from the bankruptcy court to recover property upon which they hold liens. *11 U.S.C. §§ 109(g), 362(d) and (e)*.

HOW CHAPTER 13 WORKS

A chapter 13 case begins with the filing of a petition with the bankruptcy court serving the area where the debtor has a domicile or residence. Unless the court orders otherwise, the debtor also shall file with the court (1) schedules of assets and liabilities, (2) a schedule of current income and expenditures, (3) a schedule of executory contracts and unexpired leases, and (4) a statement of financial affairs. *Bankruptcy Rule 1007(b)*. A husband and wife may file a joint petition or individual petitions. *11 U.S.C. § 302(a)*. (Official Bankruptcy Forms can be purchased at a legal stationery store. They are not available from the court.)

Currently, the courts are required to charge a $155 case filing fee and a $39 miscellaneous administrative fee. The fees should be paid to the clerk of the court upon filing or may, with the court's permission, be paid in installments. *28 U.S.C. § 1930(a); Bankruptcy Rule 1006(b); Bankruptcy Court Miscellaneous Fee Schedule, Item 8.* Rule 1006(b) limits to four the number of installments for the filing fee. The final installment shall be payable not later than 120 days after filing the petition. For cause shown, the court may extend the time of any installment, provided that the last installment is paid not later than 180 days after the filing of the petition. *Bankruptcy Rule 1006(b)*. If a joint petition is filed, only one filing fee and one administrative fee are charged.

In order to complete the Official Bankruptcy Forms which make up the petition, statement of financial affairs, and schedules, the debtor will need to compile the following information:

1. A list of all creditors and the amounts and nature of their claims;

2. The source, amount, and frequency of the debtor's income;

3. A list of all of the debtor's property; and

4. A detailed list of the debtor's monthly living expenses, *i.e.*, food, clothing, shelter, utilities, taxes, transportation, medicine, etc.

When a husband and wife file a joint petition or each spouse files an individual petition, the above detailed data must be gathered for both spouses. So that financial responsibilities can be accurately assessed when only one spouse files, the income and expenses of the non-filing spouse should be included in the debtor's schedules and statement of financial affairs.

Upon the filing of the petition, an impartial trustee is appointed to administer the case. *11 U.S.C. § 1302*. If the number of cases so warrants, the United States trustee may appoint a standing trustee to serve in all chapter 13 cases in a district. *28 U.S.C. § 586(b)*. A primary role of the chapter 13 trustee is to serve as a disbursing agent, collecting payments from debtors and making distributions to creditors. *11 U.S.C. § 1302*.

The filing of the petition under chapter 13 "automatically stays" most collection actions against the debtor or the debtor's property. *11 U.S.C. § 362.* As long as the "stay" is in effect, creditors generally cannot initiate or continue any lawsuits, wage garnishment, or even telephone calls demanding payments. Creditors receive notice of the filing of the petition from the clerk or the trustee. Further, chapter 13 contains a special automatic stay provision applicable to creditors. Specifically, after the commencement of a chapter 13 case, unless the bankruptcy court authorizes otherwise, a creditor may not seek to collect a "consumer debt" from any individual who is liable with the debtor. *11 U.S.C. § 1301.* Consumer debts are those incurred for consumer, as opposed to business, needs.

By virtue of the automatic stay, an individual debtor faced with a threatened foreclosure of the mortgage on his or her principal residence can prevent an immediate foreclosure by filing a chapter 13 petition. Chapter 13 then affords the debtor a right to cure defaults on long-term home mortgage debts by bringing the payments current over a reasonable period of time. The debtor is permitted to cure a default with respect to a lien on the debtor's principal residence up until the completion of a foreclosure sale under state law. *11 U.S.C. § 1322(c).*

The debtor must file a plan of repayment with the petition or within fifteen days thereafter, unless extended by the court for cause. *Bankruptcy Rule 3015.* The chapter 13 plan must provide for the full payment of all claims entitled to priority under section 507[1] (unless the holder of a particular claim agrees to different treatment of the claim); if the plan classifies claims, provide the same treatment for each claim within each class; and provide for the submission of such portion of the debtor's future income to the supervision of the trustee as is necessary for the execution of the plan. *11 U.S.C. § 1322.* Other plan provisions are permissive. *Id.* Plans, which must be approved by the court, provide for payments of fixed amounts to the trustee on a regular basis, typically biweekly or monthly. The trustee then distributes the funds to creditors according to the terms of the plan, which may offer creditors less than full payment on their claims. If the trustee or a creditor with an unsecured claim[2] objects to confirmation of the plan, the debtor is obligated to pay the amount of the claim or commit to the proposed plan all projected "disposable income" during the period in which the plan is in effect. *11 U.S.C. § 1325(b).* Disposable income is defined as income not reasonably necessary for the maintenance or support of the debtor or dependents. If the debtor operates a business, disposable income is defined as excluding those amounts which are necessary for the payment of ordinary operating expenses. *11 U.S.C. § 1325(b)(2)(A) and (B).*

A meeting of creditors is held in every case, during which the debtor is examined under oath. It is usually held 20 to 50 days after the petition is filed. If the United States trustee or bankruptcy administrator[3] designates a place for the meeting which is not regularly staffed by the United States trustee or bankruptcy administrator, the meeting may be held no more than 60 days after the order for relief. *Bankruptcy Rule 2003(a).* The debtor must attend the meeting, at which creditors may appear and ask questions regarding the debtor's financial affairs and the proposed terms of the plan.

11 U.S.C. § 343. If a husband and wife have filed a joint petition, they both must attend the creditors' meeting. The trustee will also attend the meeting and question the debtor on the same matters. In order to preserve their independent judgment, bankruptcy judges are prohibited from attending. *11 U.S.C. § 341(c)*. If there are problems with the plan, they are typically resolved during or shortly after the creditors' meeting. Generally, problems may be avoided if the petition and plan are complete and accurate and the trustee has been consulted prior to the meeting.

In a chapter 13 case, unsecured creditors who have claims against the debtor must file their claims with the court within 90 days after the first date set for the meeting of creditors. *Bankruptcy Rule 3002(c)*. A governmental unit, however, may file a proof of claim until the expiration of 180 days from the date the case is filed. *11 U.S.C. § 502(b)(9)*.

After the meeting of creditors is concluded, the bankruptcy judge must determine at a confirmation hearing whether the plan is feasible and meets the standards for confirmation set forth in the Bankruptcy Code. *11 U.S.C. §§ 1324 and 1325*. Creditors, who will receive 25 days' notice of the hearing, may object to confirmation. While a variety of objections may be made, the most frequent ones are that payments offered under the plan are less than creditors would receive if the debtor's assets were liquidated or that the debtor's plan does not commit all of the debtor's projected disposable income for the three-year period of the plan.

Within thirty days after the filing of the plan, even if the plan has not yet been approved by the court, the debtor must start making payments to the trustee. *11 U.S.C. § 1326(a)(1)*. If the plan is confirmed by the bankruptcy judge, the chapter 13 trustee commences distribution of the funds received in accordance with the plan "as soon as practicable." *11 U.S.C. § 1326(a)(2)*. If the plan is not confirmed, the debtor has a right to file a modified plan. *11 U.S.C. § 1323*. The debtor also has a right to convert the case to a liquidation case under chapter 7. *11 U.S.C. § 1307*. If the plan or modified plan is not confirmed and the case is dismissed, the

> If the number of cases so warrants, the United States trustee may appoint a standing trustee to serve in all chapter 13 cases in a district.

court may authorize the trustee to retain a specified amount for costs, but all other funds paid to the trustee are returned to the debtor. *11 U.S.C. § 1326(a)(2)*.

On occasion, changed circumstances will affect a debtor's ability to make plan payments, a creditor may object or threaten to object to a plan, or a debtor may inadvertently have failed

> Once the court confirms the plan, it is the responsibility of the debtor to make the plan succeed. The debtor must make regular payments to the trustee, which will require adjustment to living on a fixed budget for a prolonged period.

ceed. The debtor must make regular payments to the trustee, which will require adjustment to living on a fixed budget for a prolonged period. Alternatively, the debtor's employer can withhold the amount of the payment from the debtor's paycheck and transmit it to the chapter 13 trustee. Furthermore, while confirmation of the plan entitles the debtor to retain property as long as payments are made, the debtor may not incur any significant new credit obligations without consulting the trustee, as such credit obligations may have an impact upon the execution of the plan. *11 U.S.C. §§ 1305(c), 1322(a)(1) & 1327.*

A debtor may consent to the deduction of the plan payments from the debtor's paycheck. Experience has shown that this practice increases the likelihood that payments will be made on time and that the plan will be completed. In any event, failure to make the payments in accordance with the confirmed plan may result in dismissal of the case or its conversion to a liquidation case under chapter 7 of the Bankruptcy Code. *11 U.S.C. § 1307(c).*

to list all creditors. In such instances, the plan may be modified either before or after confirmation. *11 U.S.C. §§ 1323 & 1329.* Modification after confirmation is not limited to an initiative by the debtor, but may be at the request of the trustee or an unsecured creditor. *11 U.S.C. § 1329(a).*

MAKING THE PLAN WORK

The provisions of a confirmed plan are binding on the debtor and each creditor. *11 U.S.C. § 1327.* Once the court confirms the plan, it is the responsibility of the debtor to make the plan suc-

THE CHAPTER 13 DISCHARGE

The bankruptcy law regarding the scope of the chapter 13 discharge is complex and has recently undergone major changes. Therefore, debtors should consult competent legal counsel prior to filing regarding the scope of the chapter 13 discharge.

The chapter 13 debtor is entitled to a discharge upon successful completion of all payments under the chapter 13 plan. *11 U.S.C. § 1328(a).* The discharge has the effect of releasing the debtor from all debts provided for by the plan or disallowed (under section 502), with limited exceptions. Those creditors who were provided for in full or in part under the chapter 13 plan may no longer initiate or continue any legal or other action against the debtor to collect the discharged obligations.

In return for the willingness of the chapter 13 debtor to undergo the discipline of a repayment plan for three to five years, a broader discharge is available under chapter 13 than in a chapter 7 case. As a general rule, the debtor is discharged from all debts provided for by the plan or disallowed, except certain long term obligations (such as a home mortgage), debts for alimony or child support, debts for most government funded or guaranteed educational loans or benefit overpayments, debts arising from death or personal injury caused by driving while intoxicated or under the influence of drugs, and debts for restitution or a criminal fine included in a sentence on the debtor's conviction of a crime. *11 U.S.C. § 1328(a).* To the extent that these types of debts are not fully paid pursuant to the chapter 13 plan, the debtor will still be responsible for these debts after the bankruptcy case has concluded.

THE CHAPTER 13 HARDSHIP DISCHARGE

After confirmation of a plan, there are limited circumstances under which the debtor may request the court to grant a "hardship discharge" even though the debtor has failed to complete plan payments. *11 U.S.C. § 1328(b).* Generally, such a discharge is available only to a debtor whose failure to complete plan payments is due to circumstances beyond the debtor's control and through no fault of the debtor, after

creditors have received at least as much as they would have received in a chapter 7 liquidation case and when modification of the plan is not possible. Injury or illness that precludes employment sufficient to fund even a modified plan may serve as the basis for a hardship discharge. The hardship discharge is more limited than the discharge described above and does not apply to any debts that are nondischargeable in a chapter 7 case. *11 U.S.C. § 523.*

NOTES

1. Section 507 sets forth nine categories of unsecured claims which Congress has, for public policy reasons, given priority of distribution over other unsecured claims.

2. Unsecured debts generally may be defined as those for which the extension of credit was based purely upon an evaluation by the creditor of the debtor's ability to pay. In contrast, secured debts are those for which the extension of credit was based upon not only the creditor's evaluation of the debtor's ability to pay, but upon the creditor's right to seize pledged property on default.

3. Bankruptcy Administrators, rather than U.S. trustees, serve in the judicial districts in the states of Alabama and North Carolina.

CHAPTER 11

Reorganization Under the Bankruptcy Code

A case filed under chapter 11 of the United States Bankruptcy Code is frequently referred to as a "reorganization" bankruptcy.

HOW CHAPTER 11 WORKS

A bankruptcy case commences when a bankruptcy petition is filed with the bankruptcy court. Fed. R. Bankr. P. 1002. A petition may be a voluntary petition, which is filed by the debtor, or it may be an involuntary petition, which is filed by creditors that meet certain requirements. 11 U.S.C. §§ 301, 303. A voluntary petition should adhere to the format of Form 1 of the Official Forms prescribed by the Judicial Conference of the United States. The Official Forms may be purchased at legal stationery stores or downloaded from the Internet at www.uscourts.gov/bankform/. The voluntary petition will include standard information concerning the debtor's name(s), social security number or tax identification number, residence, location of principal assets (if a business), the debtor's plan or intention to file a plan, and a request for relief under the appropriate chapter of the Bankruptcy Code. In addition, the voluntary petition will indicate whether the debtor qualifies as a small business as defined in 11 U.S.C. § 101(51C) and whether the debtor elects to be considered a small business under 11 U.S.C. § 1121(e).

Upon the filing of a voluntary petition for relief under chapter 11 or, in an involuntary case, the entry of an order for such relief, the debtor automatically assumes an additional identity as the "debtor in possession." 11 U.S.C. § 1101. The term refers to a debtor that keeps possession and control of its assets while undergoing a reorganization under chapter 11, without the appointment of a case trustee. A debtor will remain a debtor in possession until the debtor's plan of reorganization is confirmed, the debtor's case is dismissed or converted to chapter 7, or a chapter 11 trustee is appointed. The appointment or election of a trustee occurs only in a small number of cases. Generally, the debtor, as "debtor in possession," operates the business and performs many of the functions that a trustee performs in cases under other chapters. 11 U.S.C. § 1107(a).

A written disclosure statement and a plan of reorganization must be filed with the court. 11 U.S.C. § 1121. The disclosure statement is a document that must contain information concerning the assets, liabilities, and business affairs of the debtor sufficient to enable a creditor to make an informed judgment about the debtor's plan of reorganization. 11 U.S.C. § 1125. The information required is governed by judicial discretion and the circumstances of the case. The contents of the plan must include a classification of claims and must specify how each class of claims will be treated under the plan. 11 U.S.C. § 1123. Creditors whose claims are "impaired," i.e., those whose contractual rights are to be modified or who will be paid less than the full value of their claims under the plan vote on the plan by ballot. 11 U.S.C. § 1126. After the disclosure statement is approved and the ballots are collected and tallied, the bankruptcy court will conduct a confirma-

tion hearing to determine whether to confirm the plan. 11 U.S.C. § 1128.

THE CHAPTER 11 DEBTOR IN POSSESSION

While individuals are not precluded from using chapter 11, it is more typically used to reorganize a business, which may be a corporation, sole proprietorship, or partnership. A corporation exists separate and apart from its owners, the stockholders. The chapter 11 bankruptcy case of a corporation (corporation as debtor) does not put the personal assets of the stockholders at risk other than the value of their investment in the company's stock. A sole proprietorship (owner as debtor), on the other hand, does not have an identity separate and distinct from its owner(s); accordingly, a bankruptcy case involving a sole proprietorship includes both the business and personal assets of the owners-debtors. Like a corporation, a partnership exists separate and apart from its partners. In a partnership bankruptcy case (partnership as debtor), however, the partners' personal assets may, in some cases, be used to pay creditors in the bankruptcy case or the partners may, themselves, be forced to file for bankruptcy protection.

Section 1107 of the Code places the debtor in possession in the position of a fiduciary, with the rights and powers of a chapter 11 trustee, and requires the performance of all but the investigative functions and duties of a trustee. These duties are set forth in the Bankruptcy Code and Federal Rules of Bankruptcy Procedure. 11 U.S.C. §§ 1106, 1107; Fed. R. Bankr. P. 2015(a). Such powers and duties include accounting for property, examining and objecting to claims, and filing informational reports as required by the court and the United States trustee, such as monthly operating reports. The debtor in possession also has many of the other powers and duties of a trustee including the right, with the court's approval, to employ attorneys, accountants, appraisers, auctioneers, or other professional persons to assist the debtor during its bankruptcy case. Other responsibilities include filing tax returns and filing such reports as are necessary or as the court orders after confirmation, such as a final accounting. The United States trustee is responsible for monitoring the compliance of the debtor in possession with the reporting requirements.

It should be noted that railroad reorganizations have specific requirements under subsection IV of chapter 11 which will not be addressed here and that stock and commodity brokers are prohibited from filing under chapter 11 and are restricted to chapter 7. 11 U.S.C. § 109(d).

THE SMALL BUSINESS DEBTOR

A small business debtor is defined by the Bankruptcy Code as a person engaged in commercial or business activities (not including a person that primarily owns or operates real property) that has aggregate noncontingent liquidated secured and unsecured debts that do not exceed $2,000,000. 11 U.S.C. § 101(51C). If a debtor qualifies and elects to be considered a small business under 11 U.S.C. § 1121(e), the case is put on a "fast track" and treated differently than a regular chapter 11 case under the Code. For example, the appointment of a creditors' committee and a separate hearing to approve the disclosure statement are not mandatory

in a small business case. 11 U.S.C. § 1102(a)(3). A small business case proceeds faster than a regular chapter 11 case because the court may conditionally approve a disclosure statement, subject to final approval after notice and a hearing and solicitation of votes for acceptance or rejection of the plan. Thereafter, the disclosure statement hearing may be combined with the confirmation hearing. 11 U.S.C. § 1125(f). In addition, the debtor has a shortened period of time (100 days from the date of the order for relief) within which only the debtor may file a plan. After the 100-day period expires, any party in interest may file a plan; however, all plans must be filed within 160 days from the date of the order for relief. 11 U.S.C. § 1121(e).

THE SINGLE ASSET REAL ESTATE DEBTOR

Another type of debtor that has special provisions under the Bankruptcy Code is a single asset real estate debtor. The term "single asset real estate" is defined as "a single property or project, other than residential real property with fewer than four residential units, which generates substantially all of the gross income of a debtor and on which no substantial business is being conducted by a debtor" other than operating the real property and which has aggregate noncontingent liquidated secured debts of no more than $4,000,000. 11 U.S.C. § 101(51B). The Bankruptcy Code provides circumstances under which creditors of a single asset real estate debtor may obtain relief from the automatic stay which are not available to creditors in ordinary bankruptcy cases. 11 U.S.C. § 362(d). On request of a creditor with a claim secured by the single asset real estate and after notice and a hearing, the court will grant relief from the automatic stay to the creditor unless the debtor files a feasible plan of reorganization or begins making interest payments to the creditor within 90 days from the date of the order for relief. The interest payments must be equal to the current fair market interest rate on the value of the creditor's interest in the real estate. 11 U.S.C. § 362(d)(3).

THE AUTOMATIC STAY

The automatic stay provides for a period of time in which all judgments, collection activities, foreclosures, and repossessions of property are suspended and may not be pursued by the creditors on any debt or claim that arose before the filing of the bankruptcy petition. As with cases under other chapters of the Bankruptcy Code, a stay of creditor actions against the debtor automatically goes into effect when the bankruptcy petition is filed. 11 U.S.C. § 362(a). The filing of a petition, however, does not operate as a stay for certain types of actions listed under 11 U.S.C. § 362(b). The stay provides a breathing spell for the debtor, during which negotiations can take place to try to resolve the difficulties in the debtor's financial situation.

Under specific circumstances, the secured creditor can obtain an order from the court granting relief from the automatic stay. For example, when the debtor has no equity in the property and that property is not necessary for an effective reorganization, the secured creditor can seek an order of the court lifting the stay to permit the creditor to

> While individuals are not precluded from using chapter 11, it is more typically used to reorganize a business, which may be a corporation, sole proprietorship, or partnership.

foreclose on the property, sell it, and apply the proceeds to the debt. 11 U.S.C. § 362(d).

It should be noted that, although creditors are stayed from action against the debtor unless relief is granted by the court, section 331 of the Bankruptcy Code permits applications for fees to be made by certain professionals during the case. Thus, a trustee, a debtor's attorney, or any professional person appointed by the court may apply to the court at intervals of 120 days for interim compensation and reimbursement payments. In very large cases with extensive legal work the court may permit more frequent applications. Although professional fees may be paid pursuant to authorization by the court, the debtor cannot make payments to professional creditors on prepetition obligations, i.e., obligations which arose before the filing of the bankruptcy petition. The ordinary expenses of the ongoing business, however, continue to be paid.

CREDITORS' COMMITTEES

Creditors' committees can play a major role in chapter 11 cases. The United States trustee, a federal employee to be distinguished from a private case trustee or panel trustee, appoints the committee, which ordinarily consists of unsecured creditors who hold the seven largest unsecured claims against the debtor. 11 U.S.C. § 1102. The committee may consult with the debtor in possession on the administration of the case, investigate the conduct of the debtor and the operation of the business, and participate in the formulation of a plan. 11 U.S.C. § 1103. A creditors' committee may, with the court's approval, hire an attorney or other professionals to assist in the performance of the committee's duties. A creditors' committee can be an important safeguard to the proper management of the business by the debtor in possession.

WHO CAN FILE A PLAN

There is no specific statutory time limit set for the filing of a plan; however, the debtor (unless a "small business" debtor, as set out above) has a 120-day period during which it has an exclusive right to file a plan. 11 U.S.C. § 1121(b). The debtor's exclusive period in which to file a plan may be extended or reduced by the court. After the exclusive period has expired, a creditor or the case trustee may file a competing plan. The United States trustee may not file a plan. 11 U.S.C. § 307.

A chapter 11 case may continue for many years unless the court, the United States trustee, the committee, or another party in interest acts to ensure the case's timely resolution. The creditors' right to file a competing plan provides incentive for the debtor to file a plan within the exclusive period and acts as a check on excessive delay in the case.

AVOIDABLE TRANSFERS

The debtor in possession or the trustee, as the case may be, has what are called "avoiding" powers. Such powers may be used to undo a transfer of money or property made during a certain period of time prior to the filing of the bankruptcy petition. By avoiding a particular transfer of property, the debtor in possession can cancel the transaction and force the return or "disgorgement" of the payments or property, which then are available to pay all creditors. Generally, the power to avoid transfers is effective against transfers made within 90 days prior to the filing of the petition. However, transfers to insiders (i.e., relatives, general partners, and directors or officers of the debtor) made up to a year prior to filing can be avoided. 11 U.S.C. §§ 101(31), 101(54), 547, 548. In addition, under 11 U.S.C. § 544, the trustee is given the authority to avoid transfers under applicable state law, which often provides for longer time periods. Avoiding powers are used, for example, to prevent unfair prepetition payments to one creditor at the expense of all other creditors.

CASH COLLATERAL, ADEQUATE PROTECTION, AND OPERATING CAPITAL

Although the preparation, confirmation, and implementation of a plan of reorganization is at the heart of a chapter 11 case, other issues may arise which must be addressed by the debtor in possession. The debtor in possession may use, sell, or lease property of the estate in the ordinary course of its business, without prior approval, unless the court orders otherwise. 11 U.S.C. § 363(c). If the intended sale or use is outside the ordinary course of its business, the debtor must obtain permission from the court. A debtor in possession may not use "cash collateral," i.e., collections of accounts subject to security interests or proceeds from the sale of pledged inventory or equipment, without the consent of the secured party or authorization by the court which must first examine whether the interest of the secured party is adequately protected. 11 U.S.C. § 363.

When "cash collateral" is used (spent), the secured creditors are entitled to receive additional protection under section 363 of the Bankruptcy Code. Section 363 defines "cash collateral" as cash, negotiable instruments, documents of title, securities, deposit accounts, or other cash equivalents, whenever acquired, in which the estate and an entity other than the estate have an interest. It includes the proceeds, products, offspring, rents, or profits of property and the fees, charges, accounts or payments for the use or occupancy of rooms and other public facilities in hotels, motels, or other lodging properties subject to a creditor's security interest. The debtor in possession must file a motion requesting an order from the court authorizing the use of the cash collateral. Pending consent of the secured creditor or court authorization for the debtor in possession's use of cash collateral, the debtor in possession must segregate and account for all cash collateral in its pos-

session. 11 U.S.C. § 363(c)(4). A party with an interest in property being used by the debtor may request that the court prohibit or condition this use to the extent necessary to provide "adequate protection" to the creditor.

Adequate protection may be required to protect the value of the creditor's interest in the property being used by the debtor in possession. This is especially important when there is a decrease in value of the property. The debtor may make periodic or lump sum cash payments, or provide an additional or replacement lien that will result in the creditor's property interest being adequately protected. 11 U.S.C. § 361.

When a chapter 11 debtor needs operating capital, it may be able to obtain it from a lender by giving the lender a court-approved "superpriority" over other unsecured creditors or a lien on property of the estate. 11 U.S.C. § 364.

APPOINTMENT OR ELECTION OF A CASE TRUSTEE

Although the appointment of a case trustee is a rarity in a chapter 11 case, a party in interest or the United States trustee can request the appointment of a case trustee or examiner at any time prior to confirmation in a chapter 11 case. The court, on motion by a party in interest or the United States trustee and after notice and hearing, shall order the appointment of a case trustee for cause, including fraud, dishonesty, incompetence, or gross mismanagement, or if such an appointment is in the interest of creditors, any equity security holders, and other interests of the estate. 11 U.S.C. § 1104(a). The trustee is appointed by the United States trustee, after consultation with parties in interest and subject to the court's approval. Fed. R. Bankr. P. 2007.1. Alternatively, a trustee in a case may be elected if a party in interest requests the election of a trustee within 30 days after the court orders the appointment of a trustee. In that instance, the United

> Although the appointment of a case trustee is a rarity in a chapter 11 case, a party in interest or the United States trustee can request the appointment of a case trustee or examiner at any time prior to confirmation in a chapter 11 case.

States trustee convenes a meeting of creditors for the purpose of electing a person to serve as trustee in the case. 11 U.S.C. § 1104(b).

The case trustee is responsible for management of the property of the estate, operation of the debtor's business, and, if appropriate, the filing of a plan of reorganization. Section 1106 of the Code requires the trustee to file a plan "as soon as practicable" or, alternatively, to file a report explaining why a plan will not be filed or to recommend that the case be converted to another chapter or dismissed. 11 U.S.C. § 1106(a)(5).

The court, after notice and hearing, may, at any time before confirmation, upon the request of a party in interest or the United States trustee, terminate the trustee's appointment and restore the debtor to possession and management of the property of the estate and of the operation of the debtor's business. 11 U.S.C. § 1105.

THE ROLE OF AN EXAMINER

The appointment of an examiner in a chapter 11 case is rare. The role of an examiner is generally more limited than that of a trustee. The examiner is authorized to perform the investigatory functions of the trustee and is required to file a statement of any investigation conducted. If ordered to do so by the court, however, an examiner may carry out any other duties of a trustee that the court orders the debtor in possession not to perform. 11 U.S.C. § 1106. Each court has the authority to determine the duties of an examiner in each particular case. In some cases, the examiner may file a plan of reorganization, negotiate or help the parties negotiate, or review the debtor's schedules to determine whether some of the claims are improperly categorized. Sometimes, the examiner may be directed to determine if objections to any proofs of claim should be filed or whether causes of action have sufficient merit so that further legal action should be taken. An examiner may not serve as a trustee. 11 U.S.C. § 321.

THE UNITED STATES TRUSTEE OR BANKRUPTCY ADMINISTRATOR

In addition to the case trustee or examiner and the creditors' committee, the United States trustee plays a major role in monitoring the progress of a chapter 11 case and supervising its administration. The United States trustee is responsible for monitoring the debtor in possession's operation of the business, and the submission of operating reports and fees. Additionally, the U.S. Trustee monitors applications for compensation and reimbursement by professionals, plans and disclosure statements filed with the court, and creditors' committees. The United States trustee conducts a meeting of the creditors, often referred to as the "section 341 meeting," in a chapter 11 case. 11 U.S.C. § 341. The United States trustee and creditors may question the debtor or the debtor's corporate representative under oath at the section 341 meeting concerning the debtor's acts, conduct, property, and the administration of the case.

The United States trustee also imposes certain requirements on the debtor in possession concerning matters such as reporting its monthly income and operating expenses, the establishment of new bank accounts, and the payment of current employee withholding and other taxes. By law, the debtor in possession must pay a quarterly fee to the United States trustee for each quarter of a year until the case is converted or dismissed. 28 U.S.C. § 1930(a)(6). The amount of the fee, which may range from $250 to $10,000, depends upon the amount of the debtor's disbursements during each quarter. Should a debtor in possession fail to comply with the reporting requirements of the United States trustee or orders of the bankruptcy court or fail to take the appropriate steps to bring the case to confirmation, the United States trustee may file a motion with the court to have the debtor's chapter 11 case converted to a case under another chapter of the Code or to have the case dismissed.

It should be noted that in North Carolina and Alabama, bankruptcy administrators perform similar functions that United States trustees perform in the remaining forty-eight states. The bankruptcy administrator program is administered by the Administrative Office of the United States Courts, while the United States trustee program is administered by the Department of Justice. For purposes of this fact sheet, references to United States trustees are also applicable to bankruptcy administrators.

MOTIONS

Prior to confirmation of a plan, there are several activities that may take place in a chapter 11 case. The continued operation of the debtor's business may lead to the filing of a number of contested motions. The most common are those seeking relief from the automatic stay, the use of cash collateral, or to obtain credit. There may also be litigation over executory (i.e., unfulfilled) contracts and unexpired leases and the assumption or rejection of those executory contracts and unexpired leases by the debtor in possession. 11 U.S.C. § 365. Delays in formulating, filing, and obtaining confirmation of a plan often cause creditors to file motions for relief from stay or motions to convert the case to a chapter 7 or to dismiss the case altogether.

ADVERSARY PROCEEDINGS

Frequently, the debtor in possession will institute a lawsuit, known as an adversary proceeding, to recover money or property for the estate. Adversary proceedings may take the form of lien avoidance actions, actions to avoid preferences, actions to avoid fraudulent transfers, or actions to avoid post petition transfers. Such proceedings are governed by Part VII of the Federal Rules of Bankruptcy Procedure. At times, a creditors' committee may be authorized by the bankruptcy court to pursue these actions against insiders of the debtor if the plan provides for the committee to do so or if the debtor has refused a demand to do so. Creditors may also initiate adversary proceedings by filing complaints to determine the validity or priority of a lien, to revoke an order confirming a plan, to determine the dischargeability of a debt, to obtain an injunction, or to subordinate a claim of another creditor.

CLAIMS

A claim is a right to payment or a right to an equitable remedy for a failure of performance if the breach gives rise to a right to payment. 11 U.S.C. § 101(5). In some instances, a creditor must file a proof of claim form along with documentation evidencing the validity and amount of the claim. When proofs of claim are required to be filed, creditors must file the proofs of claim with the bankruptcy clerk in the district where the case is pending. The clerk is required to keep a list of claims filed in a case when it appears that there will be a distribution to unsecured creditors. Fed. R. Bankr. P. 5003(b). Most creditors whose claims are scheduled (i.e., claims listed by the debtor on the debtor's schedules), but not listed as disputed, contingent, or unliquidated, need not file claims because the schedule of liabilities is deemed to constitute evidence of the validity and amount of those claims. 11 U.S.C. § 1111. Any creditor whose claim is not scheduled, or is scheduled as disputed, contingent, or unliquidated, must file a proof of claim in order to be treated as a creditor for purposes of voting on the plan and distribution under it. Fed. R. Bankr. P. 3003(c)(2). If a scheduled creditor chooses to file a claim, a properly filed proof of claim supersedes any scheduling of that claim. Fed. R. Bankr. P. 3003(c)(4). It is the responsibility of the creditor to determine whether the claim is accurately listed. The debtor must provide notification to those creditors whose names are added and whose claims are listed as a result of an amendment to the schedules. The notification also should advise such creditors of their right to file proofs of claim and that their failure to do so may prevent them from voting upon the debtor's plan of reorganization or participating in any distribution under that plan. When a debtor amends the schedule of liabilities to add a creditor or change the status of any claims to disputed, contingent, or unliquidated claims, the debtor must provide notice of the amendment to any entity affected. Fed. R. Bankr. P. 1009(a).

EQUITY SECURITY HOLDERS

An equity security holder is a holder of an equity security of the debtor. Examples of an equity security are a share in a corporation, an interest of a limited partner in a limited partnership, or a right to purchase, sell, or subscribe to a share, security, or interest of a share in a corporation or an interest in a limited partnership. 11 U.S.C §§ 101(16), (17). An equity security holder may vote on the plan of reorganization and may file a proof of interest, rather than a proof of claim. A proof of interest is deemed filed for any interest that appears in the debtor's schedules, unless it is scheduled as disputed, contingent, or unliquidated. 11 U.S.C. § 1111. An equity security holder whose interest is not scheduled or scheduled as disputed, contingent, or unliquidated must file a proof of interest in order to be treated as a creditor for purposes of voting on the plan and distribution under it. Fed. R. Bankr. P. 3003(c)(2). A properly filed proof of interest supersedes any scheduling of that interest. Fed. R. Bankr. P. 3003(c)(4). Generally, most of the provisions that apply to proofs of claim, as discussed above, are also applicable to proofs of interest.

CONVERSION OR DISMISSAL

A debtor in a case under chapter 11 has a one-time absolute right to convert the chapter 11 case to a case under chapter 7 unless (1) the debtor is not a debtor in possession, (2) the case originally was commenced as an involuntary case under chapter 11, or (3) the case was converted to a case under chapter 11 other than at the debtor's request. 11 U.S.C. § 1112(a). A debtor in a chapter 11 case does not have an absolute right to have the case dismissed upon request.

Generally, upon the request of a party in interest in the case or the United States trustee, after notice and hearing and "for cause," the court may convert a chapter 11 case to a case under chapter 7 or dismiss the case, whichever is in the best interest of creditors and the estate. 11 U.S.C. § 1112(b). The court may convert or dismiss a case "for cause" when there is a continuing loss to the estate, an inability to effectuate a plan, unreasonable delay that is prejudicial to creditors, denial or revocation of confirmation, or inability to consummate a confirmed plan.

There are important exceptions to the conversion process in a chapter 11 case. One exception is that, unless the debtor requests the conversion, section 1112(c) of the Code prohibits the court from converting a case involving a farmer or charitable institution to a liquidation case under chapter 7.

THE DISCLOSURE STATEMENT

The filing of a written disclosure statement is preliminary to the voting on a plan of reorganization, and the disclosure statement must provide "adequate information" concerning the affairs of the debtor to enable the holder of a claim or interest to make an informed judgment about the plan. 11 U.S.C. § 1125. After the disclosure statement is filed, the court must hold a hearing to determine whether the disclosure statement should be approved. Acceptance or rejection of a plan cannot be solicited without prior court approval of the written disclosure statement. 11 U.S.C. § 1125(b). After the disclosure statement has been approved, the debtor or proponent of a plan can begin to solicit acceptances of the plan, and creditors may also solicit rejections of the plan. Fed. R. Bankr. P. 3017(d) requires that, upon approval of a disclosure statement, the following must be mailed to the United States trustee and all creditors and equity security holders: (1) the plan, or a court approved summary of the plan; (2) the disclosure statement approved by the court; (3) notice of the time within which acceptances and rejections of the plan may be filed; and (4) such other information as the court may direct, including any opinion of the court approving the disclosure statement or a court-approved summary of the opinion. Fed. R. Bankr. P. 3017(d). In addition, the debtor must mail to the creditors and equity security holders entitled to vote on the plan or plans (1) notice of the time fixed for filing objections; (2) notice of the date and time for the hearing on confirmation of the plan; and (3) a ballot for accepting or rejecting the plan and, if appropriate, a designation for the creditors to identify their preference among competing plans. Id. However, in a small business case, the court may conditionally approve a disclosure statement subject to final approval after notice and a combined disclosure statement/plan confirmation hearing. 11 U.S.C. § 1125(F).

ACCEPTANCE OF THE PLAN OF REORGANIZATION

As noted earlier, during the first 120-day period after the filing of the voluntary bankruptcy petition, which filing also acts as the order of relief, only the debtor in possession may file a plan of reorganization. The debtor in possession has 180 days after the filing of the voluntary petition (or in a case commenced by an involuntary petition, after the order for relief) to obtain acceptances of the plan. 11 U.S.C. § 1121. For cause, the court may extend or reduce this exclusive period. 11 U.S.C. § 1121(d). The exclusive right of the debtor in possession to file a plan is lost and any party in interest, including the debtor, may file a plan if and only if (1) a trustee has been appointed in the case, (2) the debtor has not filed a plan within the 120-day exclusive period or any extension granted by the court, or (3) the debtor has not filed a plan which has been accepted by each class of claims or interests that is impaired under the plan within the 180-day period or any extensions granted by the court. 11 U.S.C. § 1121.

If the exclusive period expires before the debtor has filed and obtained acceptance of a plan, other parties in interest in a case, such as the creditors' committee or a creditor, may file a plan. Such a plan may compete with a plan filed by another party in interest or by the debtor. If a trustee is appointed, the trustee is responsible for filing a plan, a report of why the trustee will not file a plan, or a recommendation for the conversion or dismissal of the case. 11 U.S.C. § 1106(a)(5). A proponent of a plan is subject to the same requirements as the debtor with respect to disclosure and solicitation.

It should be noted that, in a chapter 11 case, a liquidating plan is permissible. Such a plan often allows the debtor in possession to liquidate the business under more economically advantageous circumstances than a chapter 7 liquidation. It also permits the creditors to take a more active role in fashioning the liquidation of the assets and the distribution of the proceeds than in a chapter 7 case.

Section 1123(a) of the Bankruptcy Code lists the mandatory provisions of a chapter 11 plan and section 1123(b) lists the discretionary provisions. Section 1123(a)(1) provides that a chapter 11 plan shall designate classes of claims and interests for treatment under the reorganization. Generally, a plan will classify claim holders as secured creditors, unsecured creditors entitled to priority, general unsecured creditors, and equity security holders.

Under section 1126(c) of the Code, an entire class of claims accepts a plan if the plan is accepted by creditors that hold at least two-thirds in amount and more than one-half in number of the allowed claims in the class. Under section 1129(a)(10), if there are impaired classes of claims, the court cannot confirm a plan unless the plan has been accepted by at least one class of non-insiders who hold impaired claims. "Impaired" claims are claims that are not going to be paid completely or in which some legal, equitable, or contractual right is altered. Moreover, under section 1126(f), holders of unimpaired claims are deemed to have accepted the plan.

Under section 1127(a) of the Bankruptcy Code, the proponent may modify the plan at any time before confirmation, but the plan as modified must meet all the requirements of chapter 11. Federal Rule of Bankruptcy Procedure 3019 provides that, when there is a proposed modification after balloting has been conducted and the court finds after a hearing that the proposed modification does not adversely affect the treatment of any creditor who has not accepted the modification in writing, the modification shall be deemed to have been accepted by all creditors who previously accepted the plan. If it is determined that the proposed modification does have an adverse effect on the claims of nonconsenting creditors, then another balloting must take place.

> In a chapter 11 case, a liquidating plan is permissible. Such a plan often allows the debtor in possession to liquidate the business under more economically advantageous circumstances than a chapter 7 liquidation.

Because more than one plan may be submitted to the creditors for approval, Federal Rule of Bankruptcy Procedure 3016(a) requires that every proposed plan and modification be dated and identified with the name

> Confirmation of a plan discharges the debtor from any debt that arose before the date of confirmation. After the plan is confirmed, the debtor is required to make plan payments and is bound by the provisions of the plan of reorganization.

of the entity or entities submitting such plan or modification. When competing plans are presented and meet the requirements for confirmation, the court must consider the preferences of the creditors and equity security holders in determining which plan to confirm.

Any party in interest may file an objection to confirmation of a plan. The Bankruptcy Code requires the court, after notice, to hold a hearing on the confirmation of a plan. If no objection to confirmation has been timely filed, the Code allows the court to determine that the plan has been proposed in good faith and according to

law. Fed. R. Bankr. P. 3020(b)(2). Before confirmation can be granted, the court must be satisfied that there has been compliance with all the other requirements of confirmation set forth in section 1129 of the Code, even in the absence of any objections. In order to confirm the plan, the court must find that (1) the plan is feasible, (2) it is proposed in good faith, and (3) the plan and the proponent of the plan are in compliance with the Code. In addition, the court must find that confirmation of the plan is not likely to be followed by liquidation or the need for further financial reorganization.

THE DISCHARGE

While some courts have a practice of issuing a discharge order in a case involving an individual, a separate order of discharge is usually not entered in a chapter 11 case. Section 1141(d)(1) specifies that the confirmation of a plan discharges the debtor from any debt that arose before the date of confirmation. After the plan is confirmed, the debtor is required to make plan payments and is bound by the provisions of the plan of reorganization. The confirmed plan creates new contractual rights, replacing or superseding pre-bankruptcy contracts.

There are, of course, exceptions to the general rule that an order confirming a plan operates as a discharge. Confirmation of a plan of reorganization will discharge any type of debtor—corporation, partnership, or individual—from most types of prepetition debts. It does not, however, discharge an individual debtor from any debt made nondischargeable by section 523 of the Bankruptcy Code. Confirmation does not discharge the debtor if the plan is a liquidation plan, as opposed to one of reorganization, and the debtor is not an individual. When the debtor is an individual, confirmation of a liquidation plan will effect a discharge unless grounds would exist for denying the debtor a discharge if the case were proceeding under chapter 7 instead of chapter 11. 11 U.S.C. §§ 1141(d)(2), 727(a).

POSTCONFIRMATION MODIFICATION OF THE PLAN

At any time after confirmation and before "substantial consummation" of a plan, the proponent of a plan may modify a plan if the modified plan would meet certain Bankruptcy Code requirements. 11 U.S.C. § 1127(b). This should be distinguished from preconfirmation modification of the plan. A modified postconfirmation plan does not automatically become the plan. A modified postconfirmation plan in a chapter 11 case becomes the plan only "if circumstances warrant such modification" and the court, after notice and hearing, confirms the plan as modified pursuant to chapter 11 of the Code.

POSTCONFIRMATION ADMINISTRATION

Federal Rule of Bankruptcy Procedure 3020(d) provides that, "[n]otwithstanding the entry of the order of confirmation, the court may issue any other order necessary to administer the estate." This authority would include the postconfirmation determination of objections to claims or adversary proceedings which must be resolved before a plan can be fully consummated. Sections 1106(a)(7) and 1107(a) of the Bankruptcy Code require a debtor in possession or a trustee to report on the progress made in implementing a plan after confirmation. A chapter 11 trustee or debtor in possession has a number of responsibilities to perform after confirmation, including consummating the plan, reporting on the status of consummation, and applying for a final decree.

REVOCATION OF THE CONFIRMATION ORDER

A revocation of the confirmation order is an undoing or cancellation of the confirmation of a plan. A request for revocation of confirmation, if made at all, must be made by a party in interest within 180 days of confirmation. The court, after notice and hearing, may revoke a confirmation order "if and only if [the confirmation] order was procured by fraud." 11 U.S.C. § 1144.

THE FINAL DECREE

A final decree closing the case must be entered after the estate has been "fully administered." Fed. R. Bankr. P. 3022. Local bankruptcy court policies may determine when the final decree should be entered and the case closed.

CHAPTER 12

Family Farmer Bankruptcy

Chapter 12 of the Bankruptcy Code was enacted by Congress in 1986, specifically to meet the needs of financially distressed family farmers. The primary purpose of this legislation was to give family farmers facing bankruptcy a chance to reorganize their debts and keep their farms.

BACKGROUND

In tailoring chapter 12 to meet the economic realities of family farming, this law has eliminated many of the barriers that family farmers had faced when seeking to reorganize successfully under either chapter 11 or 13 of the Bankruptcy Code. For example, chapter 12 is more streamlined, less complicated, and less expensive than chapter 11, which is better suited to the large corporate reorganization. In addition, few family farmers find chapter 13 to be advantageous, because it was designed for wage earners who have smaller debts than those facing family farmers. In chapter 12, Congress sought to combine the features of the Bankruptcy Code which can provide a framework for successful family farm reorganizations. At the time of the enactment of chapter 12, Congress could not be sure whether chapter 12 relief for the family farmer would be required indefinitely. Accordingly, the law (which first provided that no chapter 12 cases could be filed after September 30, 1993) currently provides that no cases may be filed under chapter 12 after January 1, 2004. As of March 2004, legislation to extend chapter 12 is pending in Congress.

The Bankruptcy Code provides that only a family farmer with "regular annual income" may file a petition for relief under chapter 12. 11 U.S.C.

§§ 101(18), 109(f). The purpose of this requirement is to ensure that the debtor's annual income is sufficiently stable and regular to permit the debtor to make payments under a chapter 12 plan. Allowance is made under chapter 12, however, for situations in which family farmers may have income that is seasonal in nature. Relief under this chapter is voluntary; thus, only the debtor may file a petition under chapter 12.

Under the Bankruptcy Code, those eligible to file as "family farmers" fall into two categories: (1) an individual or individual and spouse and (2) a corporation or partnership. Those falling into the first category must meet each of the following four criteria as of the date the petition is filed in order to qualify for relief under chapter 12.

1. The individual or husband and wife must be engaged in a farming operation.

2. The total debts (secured and unsecured) of that farming operation must not exceed $1.5 million.

3. Not less than 80% of the total debts which are fixed in amount must be related to the farming operation.

4. More than 50% of the gross income of the individual or the husband and wife for the receding tax year must have come from the farming operation.

In order for a corporation or partnership to fall within the second category of debtors eligible to file as "family farmers," the corporation or partnership must meet each of the following criteria as of the date of the filing of the petition.

1. More than one-half of the outstanding stock or equity in the corporation or partnership must be owned by one family or by one family and its relatives.

2. The family or the family and its relatives must conduct the farming operation.

3. More than 80% of the value of the corporate or partnership assets must be related to the farming operation.

4. The total indebtedness of the corporation or partnership must not exceed $1.5 million.

5. Not less than 80% of the corporation's or partnership's total debts which are fixed in amount must come from the farming operation owned or operated by the corporation or partnership.

6. If the corporation issues stock, the stock cannot be publicly traded.

HOW CHAPTER 12 WORKS

A chapter 12 case begins with the filing of a petition and several additional forms, such as schedules of assets and liabilities, a statement of financial affairs, a schedule of current income and expenditures, and a schedule of executory contracts and unexpired leases. Bankruptcy Rule 1007(b)(1). The petition and other forms are filed with the bankruptcy court serving the area where the individual lives or where the corporation or partnership debtor has its principal place of business or principal assets. The exact filing requirements in each jurisdiction are specified in local rules of court which can be obtained from the clerk's office. (Official Bankruptcy Forms can be purchased at a legal stationery store. They are not available from the court.) A husband and wife may file one joint petition. 11 U.S.C. § 302(a).

In order to complete the Official Bankruptcy Forms which make up the petition and schedules, the debtor will need to compile the following information:

1. A list of all creditors;

2. The source, amount, frequency, and reliability of the debtor's income;

3. A list of all of the debtor's property; and

4. A detailed list of the debtor's monthly farming and living expenses, i.e., food, shelter, utilities, taxes, transportation, medicine, feed, fertilizer, etc.

When a husband and wife intend to file a single, joint petition, they should gather the above-detailed data for both spouses. Even when only one spouse files, however, the income and expenses of the non-filing spouse should be included in the petition and schedules, so that the court can assess accurately the debtor's financial responsibilities.

Currently, the courts are required to charge a $200 filing fee. This fee should be paid in full upon filing or, with the court's permission, the fee for an individual debtor may be paid in up to four installments. Bankruptcy Rule 1006(b)(1). If a joint petition is filed, only one $200 fee is charged.

Upon the filing of the petition, an impartial trustee is appointed by the court or the United States trustee to administer the case. 11 U.S.C. § 1202; 28 U.S.C. § 586(b). As in chapter 13,

the trustee's primary responsibility is to act as a disbursing agent, receiving payments from debtors and making distributions to creditors.

The filing of the petition also "automatically stays" most actions by creditors to collect money or property owed to them. 11 U.S.C. § 362. Creditors, by law, generally cannot initiate or continue any lawsuits, wage garnishments, or even telephone calls demanding payment. Creditors (whose identities and mailing addresses are provided by the debtor) will receive notice of the filing of the petition from the court.

The debtor must file a plan of repayment with the petition or within 90 days afterward, unless the court determines that the need for an extension is attributable to circumstances for which the debtor should not be held accountable. 11 U.S.C. § 1221. Plans, which must be approved by the court, provide for payments of fixed amounts to the trustee on a regular basis. The trustee then distributes the funds to creditors according to the terms of the plan.

There are three types of debt: secured, priority, and unsecured. Secured debts are those for which the creditor has the right to pursue specific pledged property upon default. Priority debts are those granted special status by the bankruptcy law, such as most taxes and the costs of the bankruptcy proceeding. Unsecured debts generally are characterized as those debts for which credit was extended based solely on the creditor's assessment of the debtor's future ability to pay.

The debtor's plan usually lasts three to five years. It must provide for payment in full to all priority creditors. 11 U.S.C. § 1222(a)(2). The plan need not provide that unsecured creditors be paid in full, as long as the debtor pays under the plan all projected "disposable income" over the three to five years that the plan is in effect and as long as the plan provides that unsecured creditors are to receive at least as much as they would receive if the debtor's nonexempt assets were liquidated under chapter 7. 11 U.S.C. § 1225. "Disposable income" is defined as income which is not reasonably necessary for the maintenance or support of the debtor or his/her dependents or for the payment of expenditures necessary for the continuation, preservation, and operation of the debtor's business. 11 U.S.C. § 1225(b)(2)(A) and (B).

Secured creditors must be paid at least as much as the value of the collateral pledged for the debt. One of the features of Chapter 12 is that, in certain circumstances, payments to secured creditors can continue longer than the three-to-five-year period the plan provides for payment to unsecured and priority creditors.

Approximately 20 to 35 days after the petition is filed, a "meeting of creditors" is held. The debtor must attend this meeting, at which creditors may appear and ask questions regarding the debtor's financial affairs and the proposed terms of the plan. 11 U.S.C. § 343; Bankruptcy Rule 4002. (If a husband and wife have filed a joint petition, both must attend the creditors' meeting.) The trustee will also attend the meeting and question the debtor. In order to preserve their independent judgment, bankruptcy judges are prohibited from attending meetings of creditors. 11 U.S.C. § 341(c). Any problems with the plan are typically resolved dur-

> The debtor must file a plan of repayment with the petition or within 90 days afterward, unless the court determines that the need for an extension is attributable to circumstances for which the debtor should not be held accountable.

ing or shortly after the creditors' meeting. Generally, problems may be avoided if the petition and plan are complete and accurate and the trustee has been consulted prior to the meeting.

Within 45 days after the filing of the plan, the presiding bankruptcy judge must determine at a "confirmation hearing" whether the plan is feasible and meets the standards for confirmation under the Bankruptcy Code. 11 U.S.C. §§ 1224 and 1225. Creditors may appear at the hearing and object to confirmation. While a variety of objections may be made, the typical arguments are that payments offered under the plan are less than creditors would receive if the debtor's assets were liquidated or that the plan does not commit all of the debtor's disposable income for the three-to-five-year period of the plan.

> Upon successful completion of all payments under a chapter 12 plan, the debtor will receive a discharge which extinguishes the debtor's obligation to pay any unsecured debts that were included in the plan, even though they may not have been paid in full.

If the plan is confirmed by the bankruptcy judge, the trustee commences distribution of the funds the trustee has received from the debtor. If the plan is not confirmed, the funds paid to the trustee are returned to the debtor after deducting the trustee's percentage fee and any unpaid claim allowed for administrative expenses. 11 U.S.C. § 1226(a).

On occasion, changed circumstances will affect a debtor's ability to make payments or a debtor may inadvertently have failed to list all creditors. In such instances, the plan may be modified either before or after confirmation. 11 U.S.C. §§ 1223 and 1229.

MAKING THE PLAN WORK

Once the court confirms the plan, it is incumbent upon the debtor to make the plan succeed. The debtor must make regular payments to the trustee. Further, while confirmation of the plan entitles the debtor to retain property as long as payments are made, 11 U.S.C. § 1227(b), the debtor should not incur any significant new credit obligations without consulting the trustee, because they may impact upon the successful execution of the plan. In any event, failure to make the plan payments may result in dismissal of the case. 11 U.S.C. § 1208(c). In addition, the court may dismiss the case or convert the case to a liquidation case under chapter 7 of the Bankruptcy Code upon a showing that the debtor has committed fraud in connection with the case. 11 U.S.C. § 1208(d).

THE CHAPTER 12 DISCHARGE

As is the case under chapter 13, upon successful completion of all payments under a chapter 12 plan, the debtor will receive a "discharge" which extinguishes the debtor's obligation to pay any unsecured debts that were included in the plan, even though they may not have been paid in full. 11 U.S.C. § 1228. After the discharge has been granted, those creditors whose claims were provided for in full or in part under the plan no longer may initiate or continue any legal or other action against the debtor to collect the discharged obligations.

Certain categories of debts are not discharged in chapter 12 proceedings. 11 U.S.C. § 1228(a). Those categories include debts for alimony and child support; money obtained through filing false financial statements; debts for willful and malicious injury to person or property; debts for death or personal injury caused by the debtor's operation of a motor vehicle while the debtor was intoxicated; and debts from fraud or defalcation while acting in a fiduciary capacity, embezzlement or larceny. In fact, the discharge is more limited in chapter 12 than it is in a chapter 13 case. The bankruptcy law regarding the scope of a chapter 12 discharge is complex, however, and debtors should consult competent legal counsel in this regard prior to filing. Those debts which will not be discharged should be paid in full under a plan. With respect to secured obligations, those debts may be paid beyond the end of the plan payment period and, accordingly, are not discharged.

CHAPTER 12 HARDSHIP DISCHARGE

If payments under a plan are not completed due to circumstances for which the family farmer "should not justly be held accountable," 11 U.S.C. § 1228(b)(1), and other statutory criteria have been met, a family farmer may be excused from completing pay-ments under a plan of reorganization. If the court finds that such circumstances exist and that unsecured creditors already have received at least what they would have received if the debtor's estate had been liquidated under chapter 7 of the Bankruptcy Code, the bankruptcy court may grant the debtor a discharge of all unsecured debts provided for in the plan or disallowed by the court, with the exception of those types of debts which are excepted from discharge. Injury or illness that precludes employment sufficient to fund even a modified plan may serve as the basis for a discharge under section 1228(c). A discharge granted under section 1228(c) is often referred to as a "hardship discharge."

CHAPTER
9

Municipality Bankruptcy

In the more than 60 years since Congress established a federal mechanism for the resolution of municipal debts, there have been fewer than 500 municipal bankruptcy petitions filed. Although chapter 9 cases are rare, a filing by a large municipality can—like the 1994 filing by Orange County, California—involve many millions of dollars in municipal debt.

HISTORY OF CHAPTER 9

The first municipal bankruptcy legislation was enacted in 1934 during the Great Depression. Pub. L. No. 251, 48 Stat. 798 (1934). Although Congress took care to draft the legislation so as not to interfere with the sovereign powers of the states as guaranteed by the Tenth Amendment to the Constitution, the Supreme Court held the 1934 Act unconstitutional as an improper interference with the sovereignty of the states. Ashton v. Cameron County Water Improvement District No. 1, 298 U.S. 513 (1936). Congress enacted a revised Municipal Bankruptcy Act in 1937, Pub. L. No. 302, 50 Stat. 653 (1937), which was upheld by the Supreme Court. United States v. Bekins, 304 U.S. 27 (1938). The law has been amended several times since 1937, most recently in 1994 (amending section 109(c)) as part of the Bankruptcy Reform Act of 1994, Pub. L. No. 103–394, 108 Stat. 4106 (codified as amended at 11 U.S.C. §§ 901 to 946) (1994). In the more than 60 years since Congress established a federal mechanism for the resolution of municipal debts, there have been fewer than 500 municipal bankruptcy petitions filed. Although chapter 9 cases are rare, a filing by a large municipality can—like the 1994 filing by Orange County, California—involve many millions of dollars in municipal debt.

PURPOSE OF MUNICIPAL BANKRUPTCY

The purpose of chapter 9 is to provide a financially-distressed municipality protection from its creditors while it develops and negotiates a plan for adjusting its debts. Reorganization of the debts of a municipality is typically accomplished either by extending debt maturities, reducing the amount of principal or interest, or refinancing the debt by obtaining a new loan.

Although similar to other chapters in some respects, chapter 9 is significantly different in that there is no provision in the law for liquidation of the assets of the municipality and distribution of the proceeds to creditors. Such a liquidation or dissolution would undoubtedly violate the Tenth Amendment to the Constitution and the reservation to the states of sovereignty over their internal affairs. Indeed, due to the severe limitations placed upon the power of the bankruptcy court in chapter 9 cases (required by the Tenth Amendment and the Supreme Court's decisions in cases upholding municipal bankruptcy legislation), the bankruptcy court generally is not as active in managing a municipal bankruptcy case as it is in corporate reorganizations under chapter 11. The functions of the bankruptcy court in chapter 9 cases are generally limited to approval of the petition (if the debtor is eligible), confirmation of a plan of debt adjustment, and ensuring implementation of the plan. As a practical matter, however, the municipality may consent to have the court exercise jurisdiction in many of the traditional areas of court oversight in bankruptcy, in order to obtain the protection of court orders and eliminate the need for multiple forums to decide issues.

MEDIA INTEREST

The news media frequently is more interested in municipal bankruptcy cases than in cases filed by individuals or small businesses. As a consequence, some courts have a written policy for court personnel regarding the information that may or may not be released to the media in a case filed under chapter 9. Some courts also designate a public information officer to act as the contact person for all media inquiries concerning the municipal bankruptcy case.

ELIGIBILITY

Only a "municipality" can file for relief under chapter 9. The term "municipality" is defined in the Code to mean "political subdivision or public agency or instrumentality of a State." 11 U.S.C. § 101(40). The definition is broad enough to include cities, counties, townships, school districts, and public improvement districts. It also includes revenue-producing bodies that provide services which are paid for by users rather than by general taxes, such as bridge authorities, highway authorities, and gas authorities.

There are three additional eligibility requirements for chapter 9:

1. the entity must be specifically authorized to be a debtor under such chapter by State law or by a governmental officer or organization empowered by State law to authorize such entity to be a debtor under such chapter,

2. the municipality must be insolvent as defined in 11 U.S.C. § 101(32)(C), and

3. the municipality must desire to effect a plan to adjust such debts and either

• has obtained the agreement of creditors holding at least a majority in amount of the claims of each class that the debtor intends to impair under a plan in a case under chapter 9;

• has negotiated in good faith with creditors and has failed to obtain the agreement of creditors holding at least a majority in amount of the claims of each class that the debtor intends to impair under a plan;

• is unable to negotiate with creditors because such negotiation is impracticable; or

• reasonably believes that a creditor may attempt to obtain a preference.

11 U.S.C. § 109(c).

COMMENCEMENT OF THE CASE

Municipalities must voluntarily seek protection under the Bankruptcy Code. 11 U.S.C. §§ 303, 901(a). They may file a petition only under chapter 9. A case under chapter 9 concerning an unincorporated tax or special assessment district that does not have such district's own officials is commenced by the filing of a voluntary "petition under this chapter by such district's governing authority or the board or body having authority to levy taxes or assessments to meet the obligations of such district." 11 U.S.C. § 921(a).

A municipal debtor is required to file a list of creditors. 11 U.S.C. § 924. Normally, the list of creditors is filed with the petition. However, in some situations, the debtor may not have adequate time to prepare a list of creditors in the form and with the detail required by the Bankruptcy Rules. Thus, the Bankruptcy Rules permit the court to fix a time within which the list must be filed. Fed. R. Bankr. P. 1007.

ASSIGNMENT OF CASE TO A BANKRUPTCY JUDGE

One significant difference between chapter 9 cases and cases filed under other chapters is that the clerk of court does not automatically assign the case to a particular judge. "The chief judge of the court of appeals for the circuit embracing the district in which the case is commenced [designates] the bankruptcy judge to conduct the case." 11 U.S.C. § 921(b). This provision was designed to remove politics from the issue of which judge will preside over the chapter 9 case of a major municipality and to ensure that a municipal case will be handled by a judge who has the time and capability of doing so. S. Rep. No. 458, 94th Cong., 1st Sess. 15 (1975) (legislative history of Bankruptcy Act— Debts of Municipalities, Pub. L. No. 94–260, 90 Stat. 315 (1976)). See also S. Rep. No. 989, 95th Cong., 2d Sess. 110 (1978).

NOTICE OF CASE/OBJECTIONS/ ORDER FOR RELIEF

The Bankruptcy Code requires that notice be given of the commencement of the case and the order for relief. 11 U.S.C. § 923. The Bankruptcy Rules provide that the clerk, or such other person as the court may direct, is to give notice. Fed. R. Bankr. P. 2002(f). Such notice must also be published "at least once a week for three successive weeks in at least one newspaper of general circulation published within the district in which the case is commenced, and in such other newspaper having a general circulation among bond dealers and bondholders as the court designates." 11 U.S.C. § 923. The court typically enters an order designating who is to give and receive notice by mail and identifying the newspapers in which the additional notice is to be published. Fed. R. Bankr. P. 9008.

The Bankruptcy Code permits objections to the petition to be filed. 11 U.S.C. § 921(c). Typically, objections concern issues like whether negotiations have been conducted in good faith, whether the state has authorized the municipality to file, and whether the petition was filed in good faith. If an objection to the petition is filed, the court must hold a hearing on the objection. Id. The court may dismiss a petition if it determines that the debtor did not file the petition in good faith or that the petition does not meet the requirements of title 11. Id.

If the petition is not dismissed upon an objection, the Bankruptcy Code requires the court to order relief, allowing the case to proceed under chapter 9. 11 U.S.C. § 921(d).

AUTOMATIC STAY

The automatic stay of section 362 of the Bankruptcy Code is applicable in chapter 9 cases. 11 U.S.C. §§ 362(a), 901(a). The stay operates to stop all collection actions against the debtor and its property upon the filing of the petition. There is another provision of the Code, however, which expands the stay to entities other than the debtor. The additional automatic stay provisions under section 922(a) prohibit actions against officers and inhabitants of the debtor if the action seeks to enforce a claim against the debtor. Thus, the stay prohibits a creditor from bringing a mandamus action against an officer of a municipality on account of a prepetition debt. It also prohibits a creditor from bringing an action against an inhabitant of the debtor to enforce a lien on or arising out of taxes or assessments owed to the debtor. Section 922(d) of title 11 limits the applicability of the stay. Pursuant to that section, a chapter 9 petition does not operate to stay application of pledged special revenues to payment of indebtedness secured by such revenues. Thus, an indenture trustee or other paying agent may apply pledged funds to payments coming due or distribute the pledged funds to bondholders without violating the automatic stay.

PROOFS OF CLAIM

In a chapter 9 case, the court fixes the time within which proofs of claim or interest may be filed. Fed. R. Bankr. P. 3003(c)(3). Many creditors may not be required to file a proof of claim in a chapter 9 case. For example, a proof of claim is deemed filed if it appears on the list of creditors filed by the debtor, unless the debt is listed as disputed, contingent, or unliquidated. 11 U.S.C. § 925. Thus, a creditor must file a proof of claim, if the creditor's claim appears on the list of creditors as disputed, contingent, or unliquidated.

COURT'S LIMITED POWER

Two of chapter 9's provisions are designed to recognize the court's limited power over operations of the debtor: sections 903 and 904. Section 904 of the Code limits the power of the bankruptcy court to "interfere with (1) any of the political or governmental powers of the debtor; (2) any of the property or revenues of the debtor; or (3) the debtor's use or enjoyment of any income-producing property," unless the debtor consents or the plan so provides. The provision makes it clear that the debtor's day-to-day activities are not subject to court approval and that the debtor may borrow money without court authority. In addition, the court cannot appoint a trustee (except for limited purposes specified in section 926(a)) and cannot

> Although similar to other chapters in some respects, chapter 9 is significantly different in that there is no provision in the law for liquidation of the assets of the municipality and distribution of the proceeds to creditors.

convert the case to a liquidation proceeding. The court also cannot interfere with the operations of the debtor or with the debtor's use of its property and revenues. This is due, at least in part, to the fact that in a chapter 9 case there is no property of the estate and thus no estate to administer. 11 U.S.C. § 902(1).

Moreover, the chapter 9 debtor may employ professionals without court approval, and the only court review of fees is in the context of plan confirmation, when the court determines the reasonableness of the fees. The restrictions imposed by section 904 are necessary in order to ensure the constitutionality of chapter 9 and to avoid the possibility that the court might substitute its control over the political or governmental affairs or property of the debtor for that of the state and the elected officials of the municipality.

Similarly, section 903 of the Code states that "chapter [9] does not limit or impair the power of a State to control, by legislation or otherwise, a municipality of or in such State in the exercise of the political or governmental powers of the municipality, including expenditures for such exercise," with two exceptions—a state law prescribing a method of composition of municipal debt does not bind any nonconsenting creditor, nor does any judgment entered under such state law bind a nonconsenting creditor.

ROLE OF THE UNITED STATES TRUSTEE/ BANKRUPTCY ADMINISTRATOR

The role of the United States trustee in chapter 9 cases is typically more limited than in chapter 11 cases. Although the United States trustee appoints a creditors' committee, the United States trustee does not examine the debtor at a meeting of creditors (there is no meeting of creditors), does not have the authority to move for appointment of a trustee or examiner or for conversion of the case, and does not supervise the administration of the case. Nor does the United States trustee monitor the financial operations of the debtor or review the fees of professionals retained in the case. Bankruptcy Administrators serve a similar limited function in chapter 9 cases filed in the six judicial districts in the states of Alabama and North Carolina.

ROLE OF CREDITORS

The creditors' role is more limited in chapter 9 than in other cases. There is no first meeting of creditors and creditors may not propose a plan of adjustment. If certain requirements are met, the debtor's plan of adjustment is binding on dissenting creditors. The chapter 9 debtor has more freedom to operate without court-imposed restrictions. In each chapter 9 case, however, there is a creditors' committee that has powers and duties that are very similar to those of a committee in a chapter 11 case. These powers and duties include selecting and authorizing the employment of one or more attorneys, accountants, or other agents to represent the committee, consulting with the debtor concerning administration of the case, investigating the acts, conduct, assets, liabilities, and financial condition of the debtor, participating in the formulation of a plan, and performing such other services as are in the interest of those represented. 11 U.S.C. §§ 901(a), 1103.

INTERVENTION/RIGHT OF OTHERS TO BE HEARD

When cities or counties file for relief under chapter 9, there may be a great deal of interest in the case from entities wanting to appear and be heard. The Bankruptcy Rules provide that "[t]he Secretary of the Treasury of the United States may, or if requested by the court

shall, intervene in a chapter 9 case." Fed. R. Bankr. P. 2018(c). In addition, "[r]epresentatives of the state in which the debtor is located may intervene in a chapter 9 case. Id. In addition, section 1109 of the Bankruptcy Code permits the Securities and Exchange Commission to appear and be heard on any issue and gives parties in interest the right to appear and be heard on any issue in a case. 11 U.S.C. § 901(a). Among those that may be interested in being heard in a chapter 9 case are municipal employees, local residents, non-resident owners of real property, special tax payers, securities firms, and local banks.

POWERS OF THE DEBTOR

Due to statutory limitations placed upon the power of the court in a municipal debt adjustment proceeding, the court is far less involved in the conduct of a municipal bankruptcy case (and in the operation of the municipal entity) while the debtor's financial affairs are undergoing reorganization. The debtor has broad powers to use its property, raise taxes, and make expenditures as it sees fit. The debtor is also permitted to adjust burdensome non-debt contractual relationships under the power to reject executory contracts and unexpired leases, subject to court approval. Municipalities may also reject collective bargaining agreements and retiree benefit plans without going through the usual procedures required in chapter 11 cases. The municipality also has the authority to borrow money during a chapter 9 case as an administrative expense. 11 U.S.C. §§ 364, 901(a). This ability is important to the survival of a municipality that has exhausted all other resources. A chapter 9 municipality has the same power to obtain credit as it does outside of bankruptcy. The court does not have supervisory authority over the amount of debt the municipality incurs in its operation. The municipality also has the same avoiding powers as other debtors, may employ professionals without court approval, and fees are reviewed only within the context of plan confirmation.

DISMISSAL

As noted above, if an objection is filed, the court may dismiss the petition after notice and a hearing if the debtor did not file the petition in good faith or if the petition does not meet the requirements of chapter 9. 11 U.S.C. § 921(c). A chapter 9 case may also be dismissed, after notice and a hearing, for cause, including lack of prosecution, unreasonable delay by the debtor that is prejudicial to creditors, failure to propose a plan within the time fixed by the court, nonacceptance of a plan within the time fixed by the court, denial of plan confirmation and denial of additional time for filing another plan, material default by the debtor under a confirmed plan, or termination of a confirmed plan by reason of the occurrence of a condition specified in the plan. 11 U.S.C. § 930.

TREATMENT OF BONDHOLDERS AND OTHER LENDERS

Different types of bonds receive different treatment in municipal bankruptcy cases. General obligation bonds are treated as general debt in the chapter 9 case. The municipality is not required to make payments of either principal or interest on account of such bonds during the case. The obligations created by general obligation bonds are subject to

negotiation and possible restructuring under the plan of adjustment.

Special revenue bonds, by contrast, will continue to be secured and serviced during the pendency of the chapter 9 case through continuing application and payment of ongoing special revenues. 11 U.S.C. § 928. Holders of special revenue bonds can expect to receive payment on such bonds during the chapter 9 case if special revenues are available. The application of pledged special revenues to indebtedness secured by such revenues is not stayed as long as the pledge is consistent with section 928 [§ 922(d) erroneously refers to § 927 rather than § 928] of the Code, which insures that a lien of special revenues is subordinate to the operating expenses of the project or system from which the revenues are derived. 11 U.S.C. § 922(d).

Bondholders generally do not have to worry about the threat of preference liability with respect to any prepetition payments on account of bonds or notes, whether special revenue or general obligations. Any transfer of the municipal debtor's property to a noteholder or bondholder on account of a note or bond cannot be avoided as a preference, i.e., as an unauthorized payment to a creditor made while the debtor was insolvent. 11 U.S.C. § 926(b).

PLAN FOR ADJUSTMENT OF DEBTS

The Bankruptcy Code provides that the debtor shall file a plan. 11 U.S.C. § 941. The plan must be filed with the petition or at such later time as the court fixes. There is no provision in chapter 9 allowing creditors or other parties in interest to file a plan. This limitation is required by the Supreme Court's pronouncements in Ashton,

298 U.S. at 513, and Bekins, 304 U.S. at 27, which interpreted the Tenth Amendment as requiring that a municipality be left in control of its governmental affairs during a chapter 9 case. Neither creditors nor the court may control the affairs of a municipality indirectly through the mechanism of proposing a plan of adjustment of the municipality's debts that would in effect determine the municipality's future tax and spending decisions.

CONFIRMATION STANDARDS

The standards for plan confirmation in chapter 9 cases are a combination of the statutory requirements of 11 U.S.C. § 943(b) and those portions of 11 U.S.C. § 1129 (the chapter 11 confirmation standards) that are made applicable by 11 U.S.C. § 901(a). Section 943(b) lists seven general conditions to confirmation of a plan. The court must confirm a plan if the following conditions are met:

1. the plan complies with the provisions of title 11 made applicable by sections 103(e) and 901;

2. the plan complies with the provisions of chapter 9;

3. all amounts to be paid by the debtor or by any person for services or expenses in the case or incident to the plan have been fully disclosed and are reasonable;

4. the debtor is not prohibited by law from taking any action necessary to carry out the plan;

5. except to the extent that the holder of a particular claim has agreed to a different treatment of such claim, the plan

provides that on the effective date of the plan each holder of a claim of a kind specified in section 507(a)(1) will receive on account of such claim cash equal to the allowed amount of such claim;

6. any regulatory or electoral approval necessary under applicable nonbankruptcy law in order to carry out any provision of the plan has been obtained, or such provision is expressly conditioned on such approval; and

7. the plan is in the best interests of creditors and is feasible.

11 U.S.C. § 943(b).

Section 943(b)(1) requires as a condition to confirmation that the plan comply with the provisions of the Bankruptcy Code made applicable by sections 103(e) and 901(a) of the Code. The most important of these for purposes of confirming a plan are those provisions of section 1129 of the Code (1129(a)(2), (a)(3), (a)(6), (a)(8), (a)(10)) that are made applicable by section 901(a). Section 1129(a)(8) requires as a condition to confirmation that the plan has been accepted by each class of claims or interests that is impaired under the plan. Therefore, if the plan proposes treatment for a class of creditors such that the class is impaired (the creditor's legal, equitable, or contractual rights are altered), then that class's acceptance is required. If the class is not impaired, then acceptance by that class is not required as a condition to confirmation. Under section 1129(a)(10), the court may confirm the plan only if, should any class of claims be impaired under the plan, at least one impaired class has accepted the plan. Even if no impaired classes of creditors consent to the plan, plan confirmation is still possible under the "cram down" provisions of section 1129(b). Under "cram down," if all other requirements are met except the section 1129(a)(8) requirement that all classes either be unimpaired or have accepted the plan, then the plan is confirmable if it does not discriminate unfairly and is fair and equitable.

The requirement that the plan be in the "best interests of creditors" means something different in chapter 9 than under chapter 11. Under chapter 11, a plan is said to be in the "best interests of creditors" if creditors would receive as much under the plan as they would if the debtor were liquidated. 11 U.S.C. § 1129(a)(7)(A)(ii). Obviously, a different interpretation is needed in chapter 9 cases because a municipality's assets cannot be liquidated to pay creditors. In the chapter 9 context, the "best interests of creditors" test has generally been interpreted to mean that the plan must be better than other alternatives available to the creditors. See 4 Collier on Bankruptcy ¶ 943.03[7] (15th ed. 1994). Generally speaking, the alternative to chapter 9 is dismissal of the case, permitting every creditor to fend for itself. An interpretation of the best interests of creditors test to require that the municipality devote all resources available to the repayment of creditors would appear to exceed the standard. The courts generally apply the test to require a reasonable effort by the municipal debtor that is a better alternative for its creditors than dismissal of the case. Id.

A special tax payer affected by the plan may object to confirmation of the plan. 11 U.S.C. § 943(a). Other parties in interest may also object to confirma-

tion, including creditors whose claims are affected by the plan, an organization of employees of the debtor, and other tax payers, as well as the Securities and Exchange Commission. 11 U.S.C. §§ 1109(a), 1128(b), 901(a).

DISCHARGE

A municipal debtor receives a discharge in a chapter 9 case after (1) confirmation of the plan, (2) deposit by the debtor of any consideration to be distributed under the plan with the disbursing agent appointed by the court, and (3) a determination by the court that securities deposited with the disbursing agent will constitute valid legal obligations of the debtor and that any provision made to pay or secure payment of such obligations is valid. 11 U.S.C. § 944(b). Thus, the discharge is conditioned not only upon confirmation, but also upon deposit of the consideration to be distributed under the plan and a court determination of the validity of securities to be issued.

There are two exceptions to the discharge in chapter 9 cases. The first is for any debt excepted from discharge by the plan or order confirming the plan. The second exception is for a debt owed to an entity that, before confirmation of the plan, had neither notice nor actual knowledge of the case. 11 U.S.C. § 944(c).

At any time within 180 days after entry of the confirmation order, the court may, after notice and a hearing, revoke the order of confirmation if the order was procured by fraud. 11 U.S.C. §§ 901(a) and 1144.

The court may retain jurisdiction over the case for such period of time as is necessary for the successful implementation of the plan. 11 U.S.C. § 945(a).

Securities Investor Protection Act

SIPA

OVERVIEW

Typically, when a brokerage firm fails, the SIPC will arrange to have the failed brokerage's accounts transferred to a different securities brokerage firm. If the SIPC is unable to arrange the accounts' transfer, the failed firm is liquidated. In that case, the SIPC will send investors either certificates for the stock that was lost or a check for the market value of the shares.

Although the Bankruptcy Code provides for a stockbroker liquidation proceeding, 11 U.S.C. § 741 et seq., it is far more likely that a failing brokerage will find itself involved in a SIPA proceeding rather than a Bankruptcy Code liquidation case. Brokerage firms may be liquidated under the Bankruptcy Code, however, if SIPC does not file an application for a protective decree with the district court or if the district court finds that customers of the brokerage firm are not in need of protection under SIPA. 15 U.S.C. §§ 78eee.

HISTORY

Prior to 1938, little protection existed for customers of a bankrupt stockbroker unless they could trace cash and securities held by failed stockbrokers. In 1938 Congress enacted section 60e of the Bankruptcy Act and created a single and separate fund concept which was intended to minimize losses to customers by giving them priority over claims of gen-

Since being established by Congress in 1970, the Securities Investor Protection Corporation has protected investors who leave stocks, bonds, other securities and cash with brokerage firms by ensuring that every customer gets back what he or she left with the firm—up to $500,000 per customer, including no more than $100,000 cash. The sole function of SIPC is to return to investors securities and cash left with failed brokerages. It does not protect investors against losses in the securities markets.

eral creditors. 1898 Bankruptcy Act § 60(e)(2) (repealed). Because the fund was normally inadequate, however, customer losses continued.

Following a period of great expansion in the securities industry during the 1960's, a serious business contraction hit the industry in 1969–1970. This situation led to voluntary liquidations, mergers, receiverships, and bankruptcies of a substantial number of brokerage houses. Annotation, Validity, Construction, and Application of Securities Investor Protection Act of 1970 (15 U.S.C.S. §§ 78aaa et seq.), 23 A.L.R. Fed. 157, 179 (1975). Customers of these firms found the cash and securities which they had on deposit dissipated or tied up in lengthy bankruptcy proceedings. Along with the concern over mounting customer losses and the subsequent erosion of investor confidence, the Congress was also concerned with a possible "domino effect" involving otherwise solvent brokers that had substantial open transactions with firms that failed. In reaction to this growing concern, the Congress enacted the Securities Investor Protection Act of 1970 (hereinafter referred to as SIPA). The goal was to arrest this process, restore investor confidence in the capital markets, and upgrade the financial responsibility requirements for registered brokers and dealers. Securities Investor Protection Corp. v. Barbour, 421 U.S. 412, 414 (1975). SIPA was designed to apportion responsibility for carrying out the various goals of the legislation to several groups. Among them are the Securities and Exchange Commission (hereinafter referred to as SEC), various securities industry self-regulatory organizations, and the Securities Investor

Protection Corporation (hereinafter referred to as SIPC). SIPA was designed to create a new form of liquidation proceeding. It is applicable only to member firms and was designed to accomplish the completion of open transactions and the speedy return of most customer property. Id.

SIPA

SIPA is codified as Title 15, United States Code, Sections 78aaa–111. SIPA created SIPC, a nonprofit, private membership corporation to which most registered brokers and dealers are required to belong. 15 U.S.C. § 78ccc. The SIPC fund, which constitutes an insurance program, is authorized under 15 U.S.C. § 78ddd(a) and assessments against members are authorized by 15 U.S.C. §§ 78ddd(c) and (d). The fund is designed to protect the customers of brokers or dealers subject to SIPA from loss in case of financial failure of the member. The fund is supported by assessments upon its members. If the fund should become inadequate, SIPA authorizes borrowing against the U.S. Treasury. An analogy could be made to the role of the Federal Deposit Insurance Corporation in the banking industry.

BANKRUPTCY LIQUIDATION VERSUS SIPA LIQUIDATION IN BANKRUPTCY COURT

The essential difference between a liquidation under the Bankruptcy Code (11 U.S.C. §§ 741–752) and one under SIPA is that under the Code the trustee is charged with converting securities to cash as quickly as possible and, with the exception of the delivery of customer name securities, making cash distributions to customers of the debtor in satisfaction of their claims. A SIPC trustee, on the other hand, is required to distribute securities to customers to the greatest extent practicable in satisfaction of their claims against the debtor.

There is a fundamental difference in orientation between the two proceedings. There is a statutory grant of authority to a SIPC trustee to purchase securities to satisfy customer net equity claims to specified securities. 15 U.S.C. § 78fff–2(d). The trustee is required to return customer name securities to customers of the debtor (15 U.S.C. § 78fff–2)(c)(2)), distribute the fund of "customer property" ratably to customers (15 U.S.C. § 78fff–2(b)), and pay, with money from the SIPC fund, remaining customer net equity claims, to the extent provided by the Act (15 U.S.C. §§ 78fff–2(b) and 3(a)). A trustee operating under the Code lacks similar resources. The Code seeks to protect the filing date value of a customer's securities account by liquidating all non-customer name securities. SIPA seeks to preserve an investor's portfolio as it stood on the filing date. Under SIPA, the customer will receive securities whenever possible.

ROLE OF THE DISTRICT COURT

15 U.S.C. § 78eee(a)(3)(A) provides that SIPC may file an application for a protective decree with the United States district court if SIPC determines that any member has failed or is in danger of failing to meet obligations to customers and meets one of the four conditions specified in 15 U.S.C. § 78eee(b)(1). This application will be filed as a civil case in which SIPC or the SEC or both are named as plaintiff, and the member securities firm is named as the debtor-defendant. In the event that the SIPC refuses to act under the SIPA, the SEC may apply to the United States District Court for the District of Columbia to require the SIPC to discharge its obligations under SIPA. 15 U.S.C. § 78ggg(b). By contrast, customers of failing broker-dealers do not have an implied right of action under SIPA to compel the SIPC to exercise its statutory authority for their benefit. Barbour at 425. Upon the filing of an application, the district court has exclusive jurisdiction of the debtor-defendant and its property.

The institution of a case under SIPA brings a pending bankruptcy liquidation to a halt. Irrespective of the automatic stay, SIPC may file an application for a protective decree under SIPA. 11 U.S.C. § 742; 15 U.S.C. § 78aaa et seq. The filing stays all proceedings in the bankruptcy case until the SIPC action is completed. Id. Pending issuance of a protective decree, the district court:

[i.] shall stay any pending bankruptcy, mortgage foreclosure, equity receivership, or other proceeding to reorganize, conserve, or liquidate the debtor or its property and any other suit against any receiver, conservator, or trustee of the debtor or its property, and shall continue such stay upon appointment of a trustee …

[ii.] may stay any proceeding to enforce a lien against property of the debtor or any other suit against the debtor, including a suit by stockholders of the debtor which interferes with prosecution by the trustee of claims against former directors, officers, or employees of the debtor, and may continue such stay upon appointment of a trustee …

[iii.] may stay enforcement of, and upon appointment of a trustee ... [if a protective decree is issued] ... may continue the stay for such period of time as may be appropriate, but shall not abrogate,[sic] any right of setoff, except to the extent such right may be affected under section 553 of Title 11 of the United States Code ... and shall not abrogate the right to enforce a valid, nonpreferential lien or pledge against the property of the debtor; and

[iv.] may appoint a temporary receiver.

15 U.S.C. § 78eee(b)(2)(B)(I–iv) (emphasis added).

In addition, upon the filing of a SIPC application, 11 U.S.C. § 362 comes into effect.

SIPA provides that the district court shall issue a protective decree if the debtor consents, the debtor fails to contest the application for a protective decree, or the district court finds that one of the conditions specified in 15 U.S.C. § 78eee(b)(1) exist. If the court issues a protective decree, then the court will appoint a trustee and an attorney for the trustee whom SIPC, in its sole discretion, specifies. 15 U.S.C. § 78eee(b)(3). Upon the issuance of a protective decree and appointment of a trustee, or a trustee and counsel, the district court shall order the removal of the entire liquidation proceeding to the bankruptcy court in the same judicial district. 15 U.S.C. § 78eee(b)(4).

REMOVAL TO BANKRUPTCY COURT

The case is removed to the bankruptcy court as an adversary proceeding for liquidation. No filing or removal fee is charged. The reason for using an adversary proceeding number is historical. While these SIPA proceedings are not bankruptcy cases, by law certain procedures prescribed in chapters 1, 3, and 5, and subchapters I and II of chapter 7 of Title 11 of the United States Code are applicable in SIPA proceedings. In addition, there is no related bankruptcy case number. Statistical reports to the Administrative Office should repeat the adversary number so that the Statistics Division will know it is a SIPA matter. For adversary proceedings within the adversary SIPA proceeding, the clerk's office should use the original adversary proceeding number for the related case number.

SIPA requires that the bankruptcy court hold a hearing with 10 days notice to customers, creditors, and stockholders on the disinterestedness of the trustee or attorney for the trustee. 15 U.S.C. § 78eee(b)(6)(B). At the hearing, the court will entertain grounds for objection to the retention of the trustee or attorney for the trustee including, among other things, insider considerations. 15 U.S.C. § 78eee(b)(6)(A). If SIPC appoints itself as trustee, it should be deemed disinterested, and where a SIPC employee has been specified, the employee shall not be disqualified solely because of his employment. Id. Neither the Bankruptcy Code, Bankruptcy Rules, nor SIPA provide for United States trustee or Bankruptcy Administrator involvement.

SIPA provides for noticing of both customers and creditors. The noticing requirements provided for in 15 U.S.C.

§ 78fff–2(a)(1) are performed by the trustee, not the clerk of the bankruptcy court. While SIPA does not require a formal proof of claim for customers (other than certain insiders and their relatives), it does require a written statement of claim. The trustee will normally provide customers with claim forms and instructions. The claim form must be filed with the trustee rather than the clerk of the bankruptcy court. 15 U.S.C. § 78fff2(a)(2). With limited, specified exceptions, no claim of a customer or other creditor can be allowed unless it is received by the trustee within six months after the initial publication of notice. 15 U.S.C. § 78fff–2(a)(3).

LIQUIDATION PROCEEDINGS

The purposes of a SIPA liquidation are: (1) to deliver customer name securities to or on behalf of customers; (2) to distribute customer property and otherwise satisfy net equity claims of customers; (3) to sell or transfer offices and other productive units of the debtor's business; (4) to enforce the rights of subrogation; and (5) to liquidate the business as promptly as possible. 15 U.S.C. § 78fff(a). To the extent possible, consistent with SIPA, the liquidation is conducted in accordance with chapters 1, 3, 5 and subchapters I and II of chapter 7 of Title 11. 15 U.S.C. § 78fff(b). A section 341 meeting of creditors is conducted by the trustee. Noncustomer claims are handled as in an asset case. Costs and expenses, and priorities of distribution from the estate, are allowed as provided in section 726 of Title 11. Funds advanced by SIPC to the trustee for costs and expenses are recouped from the estate, to the extent there is any estate, pursuant to section 507 of Title 11.

> The purposes of a SIPA liquidation are: (1) to deliver customer name securities to or on behalf of customers; (2) to distribute customer property and otherwise satisfy net equity claims of customers; (3) to sell or transfer offices and other productive units of the debtor's business; (4) to enforce the rights of subrogation; and (5) to liquidate the business as promptly as possible.

POWERS OF THE TRUSTEE

The powers of the trustee in a SIPC case are essentially the same as those vested in a chapter 7 trustee appointed under Title 11. "In addition, a trustee may, with the approval of SIPC but without any need for court approval:

1. hire and fix the compensation of all personnel (including officers and employees of the debtor and of its examining authority) and other persons (including accountants) that are deemed by the trustee necessary for all or any purposes of the liquidation proceeding;

2. utilize SIPC employees for all or any purposes of a liquidation proceeding; and

3. margin and maintain customer accounts of the debtor ..."

15 U.S.C. § 78fff–1(a).

A SIPC trustee may reduce to money customer securities constituting customer property or in the general estate of the debtor. 15 U.S.C. § 78fff–1(b). The trustee shall, however, deliver securities to customers to the maximum extent practicable. 15 U.S.C. § 78fff–1(b)(1). Subject to prior approval of SIPC, but again without any need for court approval, the trustee may also pay or guarantee any part of the debtor's indebtedness to a bank, person, or other lender when certain conditions exist. 15 U.S.C. § 78fff–1(b)(2).

The trustee is responsible for investigating the acts, conduct, and condition of the debtor and reporting thereon to the court. 15 U.S.C. § 78fff–1(d)(1). The trustee must also provide a statement on the investigation to SIPC and to other persons as the court might direct. 15 U.S.C. § 78fff–1(d)(4). Moreover, the trustee must make periodic reports to the court and to SIPC on the progress of distribution of cash and securities to customers. 15 U.S.C. § 78fff–1(c).

CLAIMS

Upon receipt of a written statement of claim, the trustee promptly discharges obligations of the debtor relating to cash and securities by delivering securities or making payments to or on behalf of the customer insofar as such obligations are ascertainable from books and records of the debtor, or are otherwise established to the satisfaction of the trustee. The value of securities delivered in this regard are calculated as of the close of business on the filing date. 15 U.S.C. § 78fff–2(b).

The court must authorize the trustee to satisfy claims out of monies advanced by SIPC for this purpose, notwithstanding that the estate may not have sufficient funds for such payment. 15 U.S.C. § 78fff–2(b)(1). The court is generally not involved in the process except to the extent that a dispute arises between the trustee and customers regarding specific claims. Simple objections stay with the initial adversary proceeding. Occasionally, however, significant litigation arises in this area which generates related actions in the form of additional adversary proceedings.

DISTRIBUTION

Customer related property of the debtor is allocated as follows:

A. First, to SIPC in repayment of advances made to the extent they were used to recover securities apportioned to customer property;

B. Second, to customers of the debtor on the basis of their net equities;

C. Third, to SIPC as subrogee for the claims of customers; and

D. Fourth, to SIPC in repayment of advances made by SIPC to transfer or sell customer accounts to another SIPC member firm.

15 U.S.C. § 78fff–2(c)(1).

The trustee must deliver customer name securities to the customer if such customer is not indebted to the debtor. If indebted, then the customer may, with the approval of the trustee, reclaim securities in his name upon payment to the trustee of all such indebtedness. 15 U.S.C. § 78fff–2(c)(2).

The trustee may, with the approval of SIPC, sell or otherwise transfer to another member of SIPC, without consent of any customer, all or any part of the account of a customer. 15 U.S.C. § 78fff–2(f). The trustee may also enter into any agreement, and SIPC will advance funds as necessary, to indemnify the member firm against shortages of cash or securities in customer accounts sold or transferred. 15 U.S.C. § 78fff–2(f)(2). In addition, the trustee may purchase securities in a fair and orderly market in order to deliver securities to customers in satisfaction of their claims. 15 U.S.C. § 78fff–2(d).

To the extent customer property and SIPC advances are not sufficient to pay or satisfy in full the net equity claims of customers, then customers are entitled to participate in the estate as unsecured creditors. 15 U.S.C. § 78fff–2(c)(1).

ADVANCES

The law requires that SIPC make advances to the trustee in order to satisfy claims and otherwise liquidate the business. These advances are made to satisfy customer claims in cash, to purchase securities to satisfy net equity claims in lieu of cash, and to pay all necessary costs and expenses of administration and liquidation of the estate to the extent the estate of the debtor is insufficient to pay said costs and expenses. Any amount advanced in satisfaction of customer claims may not exceed $500,000 per customer. 15 U.S.C. § 78fff–3(a). If part of the claim is for cash, the total amount advanced for cash payment must not exceed $100,000. 15 U.S.C. § 78fff–3(a)(1). The difference between cash payments and the maximum amount allowed can be satisfied by the delivery of securities, or cash in lieu of securities.

DIRECT PAYMENT UNDER SIPA OUTSIDE THE BANKRUPTCY COURT

In certain situations, SIPC may elect to utilize a direct payment procedure to the customers of a debtor, thereby avoiding a trustee and the courts. Certain preconditions must exist. The claims of all customers must aggregate less than $250,000, the debtor must be financially distressed as defined in the law, and the cost to SIPC for direct payment process must be less than for liquidation through the courts. 15 U.S.C. § 78fff–4(a).

If direct payment is utilized, the entire proceeding remains outside the court. The process remains essentially a transaction between SIPC and the debtor's customers.

Although SIPA provides for a direct payment procedure in lieu of instituting a liquidation proceeding, the bankruptcy court may still become involved in disputes regarding the direct payment procedure. A person aggrieved by a SIPC determination with respect to a claim in a direct payment procedure may, within six months following mailing of a SIPC determination, seek a final adjudication of such claim by the court. 15 U.S.C. § 78fff–4(e). The courts having jurisdiction over cases under Title 11 have original and exclusive jurisdiction of any civil action for the adjudication of such claims. The action is to be brought in the judicial district where the head office of the debtor is located. It would be brought as an adversary proceeding in the bankruptcy court even though there is no main case.

ROLE OF SECURITIES AND EXCHANGE COMMISSION

The SEC is responsible for regulating and supervising the activities of the SIPC. The SEC promulgates operating rules which establish the role of self-regulatory organizations and examining authorities, and their reporting responsibilities to SIPC of inspections and reviews of its member firms. SIPC's member firms are also required to provide information and documentation as necessary to assist in accomplishing these inspections. The penalties for fraud, deceit, or withholding of information throughout the processes covered by this law are severe. 15 U.S.C. § 78jjj(c).

COMPENSATION IN A SIPA ACTION

SIPA specifies that the bankruptcy court must grant reasonable compensation for the services and expenses of the trustee and the attorney for the trustee. Interim allowances are also permitted. 15 U.S.C. § 78eee(b)(5)(A). Any person seeking allowances must file an application which complies in form and content with provisions in Title 11, and must also serve a copy on the debtor, SIPC, creditors and other persons the court may designate. The court is

required to fix a time for a hearing on the application. Notice need not be given to customers whose claims have been or will be paid in full or creditors who cannot reasonably be expected to receive any distribution. 15 U.S.C. § 78eee(b)(5)(B).

SIPC will review the application and file its recommendation with respect to such allowances prior to the hearing on the application. In any case where the allowances are to be paid by SIPC without reasonable expectation of recoupment and there is no difference between the amount applied for and the amount recommended by SIPC, the bankruptcy court must award that amount. 15 U.S.C. § 78eee(b)(5)(C). If there is a difference, the court must, among other considerations, place considerable reliance on the recommendation of SIPC. If the estate is insufficient to cover these awards as costs of administration, 15 U.S.C. § 78eee(b)(5)(E) provides that SIPC will advance the necessary funds to cover the costs.

Bankruptcy Terminology

ADVERSARY PROCEEDING
A lawsuit arising in or related to a bankruptcy case that is commenced by filing a complaint with the bankruptcy court.

ASSUME
An agreement to continue performing duties under a contract or lease.

AUTOMATIC STAY
An injunction that automatically stops lawsuits, foreclosure, garnishments, and all collection activity against the debtor the moment a bankruptcy petition is filed.

BANKRUPTCY
A legal procedure for dealing with debt problems of individuals and businesses; specifically, a case filed under one of the chapters of title 11 of the United States Code (the Bankruptcy Code).

BANKRUPTCY ADMINISTRATOR
An officer of the judiciary serving in the judicial districts of Alabama and North Carolina who, like the United States trustee, is responsible for supervising the administration of bankruptcy cases, estates, and trustees, monitoring plans and disclosure statements, monitoring creditors' committees, monitoring fee applications, and performing other statutory duties.

Most debtors who file bankruptcy, and many of their creditors, know very little about the bankruptcy process. The Public Information Series of the Bankruptcy Judges Division is designed to provide debtors, creditors, judiciary employees, and the general public with a basic explanation of bankruptcy and how it works. The series features eight pamphlets that discuss chapter 7 (liquidation), chapter 13 (adjustment of debts of an individual with regular income), chapter 12 (adjustment of debts of a family farmer), chapter 11 (reorganization), chapter 9 (adjustment of debts of a municipality), SIPA (the Securities Investor Protection Act), the bankruptcy discharge, and bankruptcy terminology. This pamphlet on bankruptcy terminology explains, in layman's terms, many of the legal terms that are used in cases filed under the Bankruptcy Code.

BANKRUPTCY CODE

The informal name for title 11 of the United States Code (11 U.S.C. §§ 101–1330), the federal bankruptcy law.

BANKRUPTCY COURT

The bankruptcy judges in regular active service in each district; a unit of the district court.

BANKRUPTCY ESTATE

All legal or equitable interests of the debtor in property at the time of the bankruptcy filing. (The estate includes all property in which the debtor has an interest, even if it is owned or held by another person.)

BANKRUPTCY JUDGE

A judicial officer of the United States district court who is the court official with decision-making power over federal bankruptcy cases.

BANKRUPTCY MILL

A business not authorized to practice law that provides bankruptcy counseling and prepares bankruptcy petitions.

BANKRUPTCY PETITION

A formal request for the protection of the federal bankruptcy laws. (There is an official form for bankruptcy petitions.)

BANKRUPTCY TRUSTEE

A private individual or corporation appointed in all chapter 7, chapter 12, and chapter 13 cases to represent the interests of the bankruptcy estate and the debtor's creditors.

BUSINESS BANKRUPTCY

A bankruptcy case in which the debtor is a business or an individual involved in business and the debts are for business purposes.

CHAPTER 7

The chapter of the Bankruptcy Code providing for "liquidation," i.e., the sale of a debtor's nonexempt property and the distribution of the proceeds to creditors.

CHAPTER 7 TRUSTEE

A person appointed in a chapter 7 case to represent the interests of the bankruptcy estate and the unsecured creditors. (The trustee's responsibilities include reviewing the debtor's petition and schedules, liquidating the property of the estate, and making distributions to creditors. The trustee may also bring actions against creditors or the debtor to recover property of the bankruptcy estate.)

CHAPTER 11

A reorganization bankruptcy, usually involving a corporation or partnership. (A chapter 11 debtor usually proposes a plan of reorganization to keep its business alive and pay creditors over time. People in business or individuals can also seek relief in chapter 11.)

CHAPTER 12

The chapter of the Bankruptcy Code providing for adjustment of debts of a "family farmer," as that term is defined in the Bankruptcy Code.

CHAPTER 13

The chapter of the Bankruptcy Code providing for adjustment of debts of an individual with regular income. (Chapter 13 allows a debtor to keep property and pay debts over time, usually three to five years.)

CHAPTER 13 TRUSTEE

A person appointed to administer a chapter 13 case. (A chapter 13 trustee's responsibilities are similar to those of a chapter 7 trustee; however, a chapter 13 trustee has the additional responsibilities of overseeing the debtor's plan, receiving payments from debtors, and disbursing plan payments to creditors.)

CLAIM

A creditor's assertion of a right to payment from a debtor or the debtor's property.

COMPLAINT

The first or initiatory document in a lawsuit that notifies the court and the defendant of the grounds claimed by the plaintiff for an award of money or other relief against the defendant.

CONFIRMATION

Approval of a plan of reorganization by a bankruptcy judge.

CONSUMER BANKRUPTCY

A bankruptcy case filed to reduce or eliminate debts that are primarily consumer debts.

CONSUMER DEBTS

Debts incurred for personal, as opposed to business, needs.

CONTINGENT CLAIM

A claim that may be owed by the debtor under certain circumstances, for example, where the debtor is a cosigner on another person's loan and that person fails to pay.

CREDITOR

A person to whom or business to which the debtor owes money or that claims to be owed money by the debtor.

DEBTOR

A person who has filed a petition for relief under the bankruptcy laws.

DEFENDANT

An individual (or business) against whom a lawsuit is filed.

DISCHARGE

A release of a debtor from personal liability for certain dischargeable debts. (A discharge releases a debtor from personal liability for certain debts known as dischargeable debts (defined below) and prevents the creditors owed those debts from taking any action against the debtor or the debtor's property to collect the debts. The discharge also prohibits creditors from communicating with the debtor regarding the debt, including telephone calls, letters, and personal contact.)

DISCHARGEABLE DEBT

A debt for which the Bankruptcy Code allows the debtor's personal liability to be eliminated.

DISCLOSURE STATEMENT

A written document prepared by the chapter 11 debtor or other plan proponent that is designed to provide "adequate information" to creditors to enable them to evaluate the chapter 11 plan of reorganization.

EQUITY

The value of a debtor's interest in property that remains after liens and other creditors' interests are considered. (Example: If a house valued at $60,000 is subject to a $30,000 mortgage, there is $30,000 of equity.)

EXECUTORY CONTRACT OR LEASE

Generally includes contracts or leases under which both parties to the agreement have duties remaining to be performed. (If a contract or lease is executory, a debtor may assume it or reject it.)

EXEMPT

A description of any property that a debtor may prevent creditors from recovering.

EXEMPTION

Property that the Bankruptcy Code or applicable state law permits a debtor to keep from creditors.

EXEMPT PROPERTY

Property or value in property that a debtor is allowed to retain, free from the claims of creditors who do not have liens.

FACE SHEET FILING

A bankruptcy case filed either without schedules or with incomplete schedules listing few creditors and debts. (Face sheet filings are often made for the purpose of delaying an eviction or foreclosure.)

FAMILY FARMER

An individual, individual and spouse, corporation, or partnership engaged in a farming operation who meet certain debt limits and other statutory criteria for filing a petition under chapter 12.

FRAUDULENT TRANSFER

A transfer of a debtor's property made with intent to defraud or for which the debtor receives less than the transferred property's value.

FRESH START

The characterization of a debtor's status after bankruptcy, i.e., free of most debts. (Giving debtors a fresh start is one purpose of the Bankruptcy Code.)

INSIDER (of individual debtor)

Any relative of the debtor or of a general partner of the debtor; partnership in which the debtor is a general partner; general partner of the debtor; or corporation of which the debtor is a director, officer, or person in control.

INSIDER (of corporate debtor)

A director, officer, or person in control of the debtor; a partnership in which the debtor is a general partner; a general partner of the debtor; or a relative of a general partner, director, officer, or person in control of the debtor.

JOINT ADMINISTRATION

A court-approved mechanism under which two or more cases can be administered together. (Assuming no conflicts of interest, these separate firms or individuals can pool their resources, hire the same professionals, etc.)

JOINT PETITION

One bankruptcy petition filed by a husband and wife together.

LIEN

A charge upon specific property designed to secure payment of a debt or performance of an obligation.

LIQUIDATION

A sale of a debtor's property with the proceeds to be used for the benefit of creditors.

LIQUIDATED CLAIM

A creditor's claim for a fixed amount of money.

MOTION TO LIFT THE AUTOMATIC STAY

A request by a creditor to allow the creditor to take an action against a debtor or the debtor's property that would otherwise be prohibited by the automatic stay.

NO-ASSET CASE

A chapter 7 case where there are no assets available to satisfy any portion of the creditors' unsecured claims.

NONDISCHARGEABLE DEBT

A debt that cannot be eliminated in bankruptcy.

OBJECTION TO DISCHARGE

A trustee's or creditor's objection to the debtor's being released from personal liability for certain dischargeable debts.

OBJECTION TO EXEMPTIONS

A trustee's or creditor's objection to a debtor's attempt to claim certain property as exempt, i.e., not liable for any prepetition debt of the debtor.

PARTY IN INTEREST

A party who is actually and substantially interested in the subject matter, as distinguished from one who has only a nominal on technical interest in it.

PLAN

A debtor's detailed description of how the debtor proposes to pay creditors' claims over a fixed period of time.

PLAINTIFF

A person or business that files a formal complaint with the court.

POSTPETITION TRANSFER

A transfer of a debtor's property made after the commencement of the case.

PREBANKRUPTCY PLANNING

The arrangement (or rearrangement) of a debtor's property to allow the debtor to take maximum advantage of exemptions. (Prebankruptcy planning typically includes converting nonexempt assets into exempt assets.)

PREFERENTIAL DEBT PAYMENT

A debt payment made to a creditor in the 90-day period before a debtor files bankruptcy (or within one year if the creditor was an insider) that gives the creditor more than the creditor would receive in the debtor's chapter 7 case.

PRIORITY

The Bankruptcy Code's statutory ranking of unsecured claims that determines the order in which unsecured claims will be paid if there is not enough money to pay all unsecured claims in full.

PRIORITY CLAIM

An unsecured claim that is entitled to be paid ahead of other unsecured claims that are not entitled to priority status. Priority refers to the order in which these unsecured claims are to be paid.

PROOF OF CLAIM

A written statement describing the reason a debtor owes a creditor money. (There is an official form for this purpose.)

PROPERTY OF THE ESTATE

All legal or equitable interests of the debtor in property as of the commencement of the case.

REAFFIRMATION AGREEMENT

An agreement by a chapter 7 debtor to continue paying a dischargeable debt after the bankruptcy, usually for the purpose of keeping collateral or mortgaged property that would otherwise be subject to repossession.

SECURED CREDITOR

An individual or business holding a claim against the debtor that is secured by a lien on property of the estate or that is subject to a right of setoff.

SECURED DEBT

Debt backed by a mortgage, pledge of collateral, or other lien; debt for which the creditor has the right to pursue specific pledged property upon default.

SCHEDULES

Lists submitted by the debtor along with the petition (or shortly thereafter) showing the debtor's assets, liabilities, and other financial information. (There are official forms a debtor must use.)

STATEMENT OF FINANCIAL AFFAIRS

A series of questions the debtor must answer in writing concerning sources of income, transfers of property, lawsuits by creditors, etc. (There is an official form a debtor must use.)

STATEMENT OF INTENTION

A declaration made by a chapter 7 debtor concerning plans for dealing with consumer debts that are secured by property of the estate.

SUBSTANTIAL ABUSE

The characterization of a bankruptcy case filed by an individual whose debts are primarily consumer debts where the court finds that the granting of relief would be an abuse of chapter 7 because, for example, the debtor can pay its debts.

SUBSTANTIVE CONSOLIDATION

Putting the assets and liabilities of two or more related debtors into a single pool to pay creditors. (Courts are reluctant to allow substantive consolidation since the action must not only justify the benefit that one set of creditors receives, but also the harm that other creditors suffer as a result.)

341 MEETING

A meeting of creditors at which the debtor is questioned under oath by creditors, a trustee, examiner, or the United States trustee about his/her financial affairs.

TRANSFER

Any mode or means by which a debtor disposes of or parts with his/her property.

TRUSTEE

The representative of the bankruptcy estate who exercises statutory powers, principally for the benefit of the unsecured creditors, under the general supervision of the court and the direct supervision of the United States trustee or Bankruptcy Administrator.

TYPING SERVICE

A business not authorized to practice law that prepares bankruptcy petitions.

UNITED STATES TRUSTEE

An officer of the Justice Department responsible for supervising the administration of bankruptcy cases, estates, and trustees, monitoring plans and disclosure statements, monitoring creditors' committees, monitoring fee applications, and performing other statutory duties.

UNDERSECURED CLAIM

A debt secured by property that is worth less than the amount of the debt.

UNLAWFUL DETAINER ACTION

A lawsuit brought by a landlord against a tenant to evict the tenant from rental property—usually for nonpayment of rent.

UNLIQUIDATED CLAIM

A claim for which a specific value has not been determined.

UNSCHEDULED DEBT

A debt that should have been listed by a debtor in the schedules filed with the court but was not. (Depending on the circumstances, an unscheduled debt may or may not be discharged.)

UNSECURED CLAIM

A claim or debt for which a creditor holds no special assurance of payment, such as a mortgage or lien; a debt for which credit was extended based solely upon the creditor's assessment of the debtor's future ability to pay.

VOLUNTARY TRANSFER

A transfer of a debtor's property with the debtor's consent.

SOURCES

Doran, *Personal Bankruptcy and Debt Adjustment*, 135–139 (1991)

Griffin, *Personal Bankruptcy: What You Should Know*, 145–149 (1994)

Questions and Answers

What Every Investor Should Know ...

Corporate Bankruptcy

What happens when a public company files for protection under the federal bankruptcy laws? Who protects the interests of investors? Do the old securities have any value when, and if, the company is reorganized? We hope this information answers these and other frequently asked questions about the lengthy and sometimes uncertain bankruptcy process.

What Happens to the Company?

Federal bankruptcy laws govern how companies go out of business or recover from crippling debt. A bankrupt company, the "debtor," might use **Chapter 11** of the Bankruptcy Code to "reorganize" its business and try to become profitable again. Management continues to run the day-to-day business operations but all significant business decisions must be approved by a bankruptcy court.

Under **Chapter 7**, the company stops all operations and goes completely out of business. A trustee is appointed to "liquidate" (sell) the company's assets and the money is used to pay off the debt, which may include debts to creditors and investors.

The investors who take the least risk are paid first. For example, secured creditors take less risk because the credit that they extend is usually backed by collateral, such as a mortgage or other assets of the company. They know they will get paid first if the company declares bankruptcy.

Bondholders have a greater potential for recovering their losses than stockholders, because bonds represent the debt of the company and the company has agreed to pay bondholders interest and to return their principal. Stockholders own the company, and take greater risk. They could make more money if the company does well, but they could lose money if the company does poorly. The owners are last in line to be repaid if the company fails. Bankruptcy laws determine the order of payment.

How Are Assets Divided in Bankruptcy?

Secured Creditors - often a bank, is paid first.

Unsecured Creditors - such as banks, suppliers, and bondholders, have the next claim.

Stockholders - owners of the company, have the last claim on assets and may not receive anything if the Secured and Unsecured Creditors' claims are not fully repaid.

What Will Happen to My Stock or Bond?

A company's securities may continue to trade even after the company has filed for bankruptcy under Chapter 11. In most instances, companies that file under Chapter 11 of the Bankruptcy Code are generally unable to meet the listing standards to continue to trade on Nasdaq or the New York Stock Exchange. However, even when a company is delisted from one of these major stock exchanges, their shares may continue to trade on either the OTCBB or the Pink Sheets. There is no federal law that prohibits trading of securities of companies in bankruptcy.

Note: Investors should be cautious when buying common stock of companies in Chapter 11 bankruptcy. It is extremely risky and is likely to lead to financial loss. Although a company may emerge from bankruptcy as a viable entity, generally, the creditors and the bondholders become the new owners of the shares. **In most instances, the company's plan of reorganization will cancel the existing equity shares.** This happens in bankruptcy cases because secured and unsecured creditors are paid from the company's assets before common stockholders. And in situations where shareholders do participate in the plan, their shares are usually subject to substantial dilution.

If the company does come out of bankruptcy, there may be two different types of common stock, with different ticker symbols, trading for the same company. One is the old common stock (the stock that was on the market when the company went into bankruptcy), and the second is the new common stock that the company issued as part of its reorganization plan. If the old common stock is traded on the OTCBB or on the Pink Sheets, it will have a five-letter ticker symbol that ends in "Q," indicating that the stock was involved with bankruptcy proceedings. The ticker symbol for the new common stock will not end in "Q". Sometimes the new stock may not have been issued by the company, although it has been authorized. In that situation, the stock is said to be trading "when issued," which is shorthand for "when, as, and if issued." The ticker symbol of stock that is trading "when issued" will end with a "V". Once the company actually issues the newly authorized stock, the "V" will no longer appear at the end of the ticker symbol. Be sure you know which shares you are purchasing, because the old shares that were issued before the company filed for bankruptcy may be worthless if the company has emerged from bankruptcy and has issued new common stock.

During bankruptcy, bondholders will stop receiving interest and principal payments, and stockholders will stop receiving dividends. If you are a bondholder, you may receive new stock in exchange for your bonds, new bonds, or a combination of stock and bonds. If you are a stockholder, the trustee may ask you to send back your old stock in exchange for new shares in the reorganized company. The new shares may be fewer in number and may be worth less than your old shares. The reorganization plan will spell out your rights as an investor, and what you can expect to receive, if anything, from the company.

The bankruptcy court may determine that stockholders don't get anything because the debtor is insolvent. (A debtor's solvency is determined by the difference between the value of its assets and its liabilities.) If the company's liabilities are greater than its assets, your stock may be worthless. Contact your local Internal Revenue Service (IRS) office or call 1-800-829-1040 for information about how to report worthless securities as a loss on your income tax return. If you don't know whether your stock has value, and you can't find a stock or bond price in the newspaper, ask your broker or the company for information.

"Prepackaged Bankruptcy Plans"

Sometimes companies prepare a reorganization plan that is negotiated and voted on by creditors and stockholders before they actually file for bankruptcy. This shortens and simplifies the process, saving the company money. For example, Resorts International and TWA used this method.

If prepackaged plans involve an offer to sell a security, they may have to be registered with the SEC. You will get a prospectus and a ballot, and it's important to vote if you want to have any impact on the process. Under the Bankruptcy Code, two-thirds of the stockholders who vote must accept the plan before it can be implemented, and dissenters will have to go along with the majority.

Why Would a Company Choose Chapter 11?

Most publicly-held companies will file under Chapter 11 rather than Chapter 7 because they can still run their business and control the bankruptcy process. Chapter 11 provides a process for rehabilitating the company's faltering business. Sometimes the company successfully works out a plan to return to profitability; sometimes, in the end, it liquidates. Under a Chapter 11 reorganization, a company usually keeps doing business and its stock and bonds may continue to trade in our securities markets. Since they still trade, the company must continue to file SEC reports with information about significant developments. For example, when a company declares bankruptcy, or has other significant corporate changes, they must report it within 15 days on the SEC's Form 8-K.

How Does Chapter 11 Work?

The U.S. Trustee, the bankruptcy arm of the Justice Department, will appoint one or more committees to represent the interests of creditors and stockholders in working with the company to develop a plan of reorganization to get out of debt. The plan must be accepted by the creditors, bondholders, and stockholders, and confirmed by the court. However, even if creditors or stockholders vote to reject the plan, the court can disregard the vote and still confirm the plan if it finds that the plan treats creditors and stockholders fairly. Once the plan is confirmed, another more detailed report must be filed with the SEC on Form 8-K. This report must contain a summary of the plan, but sometimes a copy of the complete plan is attached.

Who Develops the Reorganization Plan for the Company?

Committees of creditors and stockholders negotiate a plan with the company to relieve the company from repaying part of its debt so that the company can try to get back on its feet.

- One committee that must be formed is called the "official committee of unsecured creditors." They represent all unsecured creditors, including bondholders. The "indenture trustee," often a bank hired by the company when it originally issued a bond, may sit on the committee.

- An additional official committee may sometimes be appointed to represent stockholders.

- The U.S. Trustee may appoint another committee to represent a distinct class of creditors, such as secured creditors, employees or subordinated bondholders.

After the committees work with the company to develop a plan, the bankruptcy court must find that it legally complies with the Bankruptcy Code before the plan can be implemented. This process is known as plan confirmation and is usually completed in a few months.

Steps in Development of the Plan:

- The debtor company develops a plan with committees.

- Company prepares a disclosure statement and reorganization plan and files it with the court.

- SEC reviews the disclosure statement to be sure it's complete.

- Creditors (and sometimes the stockholders) vote on the plan.

- Court confirms the plan, and

- Company carries out the plan by distributing the securities or payments called for by the plan.

What is the Role of the U.S. Securities & Exchange Commission in Chapter 11 Bankruptcies?

Generally, the SEC's role is limited. The SEC will:

- review the disclosure document to determine if the company is telling investors and creditors the important information they need to know; and

- ensure that stockholders are represented by an official committee, if appropriate.

Although the SEC does not negotiate the economic terms of reorganization plans, we may take a position on important legal issues that will affect the rights of public investors in other bankruptcy cases as well. For example, the SEC may step in if we believe that the company's officers and directors are using the bankruptcy laws to shield themselves from lawsuits for securities fraud.

How Will I Know What's Going On?

Sometimes, you may first learn about a bankruptcy in the news. If you hold stock or bonds in street name with a broker, your broker should forward information from the company to you. If you hold a stock or bond in your own name, you should receive information directly from the company.

You may be asked to vote on the plan of reorganization, although you may not get the full value of your investment back. In fact, sometimes stockholders don't get anything back, and they don't get to vote on the plan.

Before you vote, you should receive from the company:

- a copy of the reorganization plan or a summary;

- a court approved disclosure statement which includes information to help you make an informed judgment about the plan;

- a ballot to vote on the plan; and

- notice of the date, if any, for a hearing on the court's confirmation of the plan, including the deadline for filing objections.

Even when stockholders do not vote, they should get a summary of the disclosure statement, and a notice on how to file an objection to the plan.

Stockholders may also receive other notices unrelated to the plan of reorganization, such as a notice of a hearing on the proposed sale of the debtor's assets, or notice of a hearing if the company converts to a Chapter 7 bankruptcy.

What is Chapter 7 Bankruptcy?

Some companies are so far in debt or have other problems so serious that they can't continue their business operations. They are likely to "liquidate" and file under Chapter 7. Their assets are sold for cash by a court appointed trustee. Administrative and legal expenses are paid first, and the remainder goes to creditors. Secured creditors will have their collateral returned to them. If the value of the collateral is not sufficient to repay them in full, they will be grouped with other unsecured creditors for the rest of their claim. Bondholders, and other unsecured creditors, will be notified of the Chapter 7, and should file a claim in case there's money left for them to receive a payment.

Stockholders do not have to be notified of the Chapter 7 case because they generally don't receive anything in return for their investment. But, in the unlikely event that creditors are paid in full, stockholders will be notified and given an opportunity to file claims.

Does My Stock or Bond Have Any Value?

Usually, the stock of a Chapter 7 company is worthless and you have lost the money you invested.

If you hold a bond, you might only receive a fraction of its face value. It will depend on the amount of assets available for distribution and where your debt ranks in the priority list on the first page. If your bond is secured by collateral, your payment will depend in large part on the value of the collateral.

Where Can I Find More Information?

The Company. - Contact the investor relations department in the company's home office. They can give you more information on the bankruptcy proceeding, including the name, address, and phone number of the court handling the bankruptcy.

Your Broker. - If you can't find information in the newspaper or the library, or you haven't received any correspondence from the company, call the person who sold you the investment.

The SEC. - Companies file regular reports with the SEC in a computer database known as EDGAR. For example, a company declaring bankruptcy will file a form 8-K that tells where the case is pending and which chapter of bankruptcy was filed. You can access EDGAR through your computer at: http://www.sec.gov

Bankruptcy Court. - If the company is in Chapter 7, and has not filed reports with the SEC, or you need more information, the bankruptcy court itself is another source. This court is usually located where the company has its main place of business or where the company is incorporated. (There is at least one bankruptcy court in each state and the District of Columbia.) Once you know a company's main place of business or state of incorporation, you can obtain the address and phone number of the bankruptcy court for that region by visiting the website of the Administrative Office of the United States Courts or by calling (202) 502-1900. Court addresses and phone numbers are also listed in the publication, The American Bench, which you can find at your local library. In addition, you'll find links to U.S. Bankruptcy Court websites at http://www.uscourts.gov/bankruptcycourts.html.

U.S. Trustee at the Department of Justice. - The U.S. Trustee has broad administrative responsibilities in bankruptcy cases. Check the U.S. Trustee's website, your local telephone book, or the public library for the field office closest to you, and contact them for information on the status of the bankruptcy.

A Securities or Bankruptcy Attorney. - You may want to talk to an attorney, especially if you believe that the debtor defrauded you and you want to know your legal options. If you suspect fraud, you should also report it to the SEC or your state securities regulator.

BN Publishing

Improving People's Life

www.bnpublishing.net

Recommended Readings

• Technical Analysis of Stock Trends, Robert D. Edwards, John Magee, www.bnpublishing.net

• Wall Street: The Other Las Vegas, Nicolas Darvas, www.bnpublishing.net

• The Anatomy of Success, Nicolas Darvas, www.bnpublishing.net

• The Dale Carnegie Course on Effective Speaking, Personality Development, and the Art of How to Win Friends & Influence People, Dale Carnegie, www.bnpublishing.net

• The Law of Success In Sixteen Lessons by Napoleon Hill (Complete, Unabridged), Napoleon Hill, www.bnpublishing.net

• It Works, R. H. Jarrett, www.bnpublishing.net

• Darvas System for Over the Counter Profits, Nicolas Darvas, www.bnpublishing.net

• The Art of Public Speaking (Audio CD), Dale Carnegie, wwww.bnpublishing.net

• The Success System That Never Fails (Audio CD), W. Clement Stone, www.bnpublishing.net

BN Publishing

Improving People's Life

www.bnpublishing.net

9 781607 960140